Teenage Depression

Teenage Depression

A CBT Guide for Parents

Monika Parkinson
and
Shirley Reynolds

ROBINSON

ROBINSON

First published in Great Britain in 2015 by Robinson

Important note
This book is not intended as a substitute for medical advice or
treatment. Any person with a condition requiring medical attention
should consult a qualified medical practitioner or suitable therapist.

A CIP catalogue record for this book
is available from the British Library.

ISBN 978-1-47211-454-9 (paperback)
ISBN: 978-1-47211-455-6 (ebook)

Typeset in Gentium by Initial Typesetting Services, Edinburgh
Printed and bound in Great Britain by Clays Ltd, St Ives plc

Papers used by Robinson are from well-managed forests and
other responsible sources

MIX
Paper from
responsible sources
FSC
www.fsc.org   FSC® C104740

Robinson
is an imprint of
Little, Brown Book Group
Carmelite House
50 Victoria Embankment
London EC4Y 0DZ

An Hachette UK Company
www.hachette.co.uk

www.littlebrown.co.uk

Acknowledgements

Using Cognitive Behaviour Therapy (CBT) to tackle depression and low mood is all about collaboration and partnership. This book has been written with that backdrop. We have been so lucky to collaborate with many inspirational, generous and compassionate people.

In a book like this, which is not written for an academic audience, it is not appropriate to exhaustively cite every influence. We are not even sure we are consciously aware of each and every influence – we have absorbed so much from so many that it becomes impossible to know what idea, what thought, or what insight comes from whom. CBT draws on many different ideas in psychology, it tries to help us make sense of the complex humans that we are, and to find solutions to the problems we face in life. As an academic subject in psychology it is fascinating and tantalizing. CBT has impacted on and inspired the whole field of psychotherapy by putting itself on the line, welcoming critical, high-quality research, and continually developing, improving and innovating.

However, CBT really only comes alive when it is put into action. And, as ever, it is people, always people, who bring it to life.

The first people we need to thank are the many individuals with whom we have worked clinically over many years. They have generously and bravely allowed us to share a part of their lives, to work with them and to learn from their experiences. We hope this book will help others, whom we will never meet, to share in some of that background and learning. We now have pretty good evidence that using CBT techniques, as self-help, can reduce the symptoms of low mood and depression. We hope that this book, written specifically for the parents of young people who feel low and sad, will be useful to them.

We have many dear colleagues to thank. Paul Gilbert is a psychological tour de force. His ideas about the critical role of self-compassion have influenced so many of us, in so many ways, large and small. In his curiosity, openness to experience, kindness and tolerance he also personifies the theories he developed. Colleagues at the Sheffield MRC/ESRC Social and Applied Psychology Unit were staunchly out at the front of scientific research into psychotherapy, looking at what it was and how it worked at a time when psychotherapy was generally thought of as an indulgence rather than the essential component of effective healthcare it is today. The late Malcolm Adams was an early, wise and supportive mentor. Malcolm always promoted the model of the scientist practitioner. For him this was not a sound bite – he truly valued the importance of rigorously testing our ideas and theories in real life, with real problems and with real people.

Our colleagues at the University of Reading, at the Charlie Waller Institute, and the Winnicott Research Unit have created a fantastic, stimulating and enjoyable working environment. The School of Psychology and Clinical Language Sciences has encouraged us to look around at the many links between CBT and the rest of academic psychology. It is through exploiting links with the science of psychology and neuroscience, and continuing to develop its basic science, that CBT will continue to flourish.

We enjoy a very close relationship with our NHS colleagues. Despite the real and unrelenting pressures on services, the financial cutbacks, and the rising demand for their services for children, young people and families, our friends working in the NHS continue to provide their very best, to many, at all times. The NHS is an amazing organization, the best in the world. We, and so many millions of other people, are in its debt.

We would like to thank the parents and colleagues who have provided input and have helped us with earlier drafts of the book. We particularly wish to thank Anna Zajac, Dr Cyra Neave, Dr Jenna Lova, Dr Georgina Clifford, Janet Goldsworthy and Gary Parkinson for their incredibly valuable input. The success of the *Overcoming Your Child's Fears and Worries* self-help book for parents, written by Dr Lucy Willetts and Dr Cathy Creswell, and proven subsequently to be clinically effective, also played an important part in inspiring this book. Our appreciation also goes to Andrew McAleer and Fritha Saunders of Constable & Robinson. The Charlie Waller Memorial Trust provided financial and moral support to Shirley Reynolds. The Trust works to raise awareness of depression and fights stigma. This book is written with those same aims and values.

Finally, we would like to thank our wonderful families for their never-ending support, encouragement, inspiration and understanding.

Follow Shirley on Twitter at @sci_pract
and The Charlie Walker Institute at @CharlieWalkerIn

Contents

Part 1

Introduction to low mood and depression in teenagers

1

Introduction

As a parent, picking up a book such as this one may not be easy. It is likely that the reason you are reading this is because your child is struggling with their mood in one way or another and you are looking for ways to help him or her. Acknowledging that your child is struggling and may need extra help can be difficult because, ultimately, most parents want their children to be happy, carefree and to enjoy their life as much as possible. Realizing that your child may be unhappy will be very worrying for many parents.

You may be wondering how this situation came about. Is it something that runs in the family? Was it something about your child's friendships or time at school? Is it something to do with their early upbringing? Did the family and child experience hardships? Or, you may be asking yourself, 'Is it something that I did?' These are very common questions that many parents ask, and parents often blame themselves for their child's difficulties. Despite the fact that most parents do everything they can in order to do the best for their children, when things go wrong, they often direct the blame towards themselves. How many times do parents congratulate themselves when their children are doing well? Somehow it's easier to feel responsible for the negative things compared to the positive things. Depression is a complex illness and it is rarely caused by one thing or event. **It is very unlikely to be anyone's fault!** While it can be useful to develop a better understanding of what led to the problems, and we help you to do this in one of the chapters in this book, it is even more useful to work out what might be keeping the problems going right now. Having a good understanding of the things that are maintaining the difficulties means we have the power to do something about them and to make positive changes.

This book will help you to understand what depression is and to determine whether your child is experiencing depression. There are suggestions and guidelines for questions to ask and how to put in place safety measures. The majority of the book is focused on helping you to discover what may be maintaining your child's depressed mood, with suggestions for strategies and ideas for overcoming this.

Along with this book there is also an accompanying book available for teenagers to read – *Am I Depressed and What Can I Do About It?* The book helps teenagers to better understand what depression is and how it may be affecting them. The same teenagers that are introduced in this book also appear in the teenager's book, along with their parents. It also contains self-help strategies for teenagers to use themselves to feel better. If you think your child would find it helpful to have their own version of the book to read then please let them know about the companion book, or you could buy it for them.

Parent reflections:

'It's not easy. Parenting a depressed teenager is not easy. You need to know that! But you can do it!'

'I became very isolated when my child was depressed. There was little support for me as a mum. Mental illness is still hard to talk about in our society. If you are brave enough to open up sometimes you can get a hurtful response at the point when you are least able to cope with it. People may not understand how it is affecting you. They may not see how your family struggles to cope. They may not realize that your child is ill. Just be aware of the ignorance that persists and be aware that there's not much you can do about it at the time. Also be aware that no one is to blame. It is nobody's fault.'

How common is depression in teenagers?

Many studies and surveys tell us that depression in teenagers is very common. About a quarter of all teenagers will have experienced depression by the time they are nineteen years old. At any one time, in a group of a hundred teenagers, around five or six of them will be experiencing depression (and it is likely to be more since it's very difficult to know about everyone who is affected). While these are unfortunate statistics for young people on the whole, it also means that you are not alone with the worries you are having about your child. It is likely that many other teenagers and parents, perhaps at your child's school and in your neighbourhood, will be going through similar experiences. Depression does not discriminate between race, ethnic backgrounds or social class. It can strike anyone at any time of their life and it does not mean that the individual is weak or a failure in any way. Depression does seem to affect more teenagers than younger children, which may be related to the many changes that teenagers go through as they mature into adults. Fortunately, once we know we are dealing with depression, there are many things that can be done to help teenagers to overcome their low mood.

What is depression?

It's important to remember that depression as an illness is not the same as the term we sometimes use to describe a temporary emotional state such as sadness or feeling low. People use the term 'depressed' to describe how they may be feeling on a given day or part of the day. It is an interesting contradiction that the word 'depression' can still have such stigma attached to it, yet the word 'depressed' is used all the time by the general public. There is often confusion about what depression is. This is not something that is discussed regularly or openly by people outside of the mental health and healthcare fields. In fact, many parents say that they have found that depression is still a taboo subject. The impact of this is that young people, parents and families can be left feeling quite lonely and isolated with the problem, with little understanding from their wider family, friends and, at times, their child's school and community. It can be so difficult to explain to others what it's like to support a child with depression on a daily basis. How do you begin to explain the way it impacts on the family or all the concerns that you have about your child's wellbeing and future?

Having depression is a serious matter. It can affect every aspect of a person's life, from the quality of their sleep to the quality of their relationships. It is often invisible. While someone with a broken leg goes through many difficulties associated with not being able to move around freely and being in pain, it is something that is very visible. This means that others around that person can immediately appreciate some of the struggles of being in this position, and people often make allowances to help the person cope. Depression is not only hard to spot, it is often actively hidden. In extreme cases people who are depressed resort to extreme coping behaviours, such as self-harm or suicide attempts.

Because depression is often hidden, young people with depression frequently suffer in silence for significant periods of time. Sometimes this is also the case for the young person's immediate family. For families who are yet to receive support and treatment it can feel like they are on a desert island, with little idea of how to move forward. It can be a huge relief when others start talking to the young person and their family about how they are feeling and the impact that being depressed is having on their life.

How do I know my child has depression?

Most parents know when their child is not OK. They may be generally sad and withdrawn, or spending most of their time in their room, may be snappy or getting into arguments with family members more often, not eating well, not wanting to go out or do things with the family or others, getting into trouble at school or showing other, more concerning behaviours. It can be difficult, however, for some parents to know whether this is usual teenage behaviour, perhaps a phase their child is going through, or something more serious such as depression. Some parents may already know that their child has depression and some families may have already discussed this with their GP or other professionals. Indeed, some parents may have already dealt with other members of the family who have been depressed or have experienced it themselves. If you are a parent wondering whether your child is depressed, the following section will outline the common symptoms of depression, and hopefully give you a clearer understanding of what might be going on for your child (the symptoms should only be counted if it is a definite departure from your child's usual behaviour and personality).

Symptoms of depression

Core symptoms

Feeling low or unhappy a lot of the time

Loss of interest in and enjoyment of usual activities

Irritable mood

Other main symptoms

Feeling irritable or angry

Changes in sleeping habits (sleeping much more than usual/

difficulty falling or staying asleep)

Feeling worthless

Tiredness, reduced energy

Big changes in weight

Feeling inappropriate guilt

Changes in appetite

Difficulties with making decisions

Difficulties with concentration

Feeling restless or agitated

Being much more slowed down

Feeling hopeless about the future

Thoughts of death

Thoughts of self-harm

Thoughts about suicide or actual suicide attempts

Additional possible signs of depression

Feelings of loneliness

Frequent tearfulness

Feeling unable to cry

Feeling numb or empty or unable to feel emotions

Feeling unable to cope

Lacking motivation or inability to start activities

Feeling trapped

Loss of confidence

Physical symptoms such as aches and pains

Wanting to be alone much of the time

Urges to self-harm or actual self-harming behaviours

If you are concerned that your child may have depression it will be very important for them to receive the right support as soon as possible. A visit to the GP will help you to determine the extent of the problem. It might also be a good idea to monitor his or her symptoms for about one or two weeks. You can do this together with your child or if you prefer not to discuss this openly just yet then you can do this on your own to begin with. Some of the symptoms will be more visible (e.g. tearfulness, irritability), and others are much more private (e.g. feeling hopeless about the future) and therefore you may need to ask your child some questions to get a better idea of some of these feelings.

Please remember that it is important to receive the right professional support as soon as possible so that you do not feel that you are dealing with this on your own. There is information here to help you understand your child's depression but we do not encourage parents to make diagnoses on their own.

Using self-report questionnaires

Many doctors and therapists use self-report questionnaires (or parent-report questionnaires) to help them assess whether someone has depression. We have included one of these below just in case you may wish to use this with your child. The questionnaire can also be useful to monitor whether your child's depression is getting worse, staying the same, or hopefully getting better. If you decide to try this questionnaire, we suggest you use it every two weeks or so to monitor change.

Please do not feel that you need to be using this questionnaire with your child. It is included here simply for those of you who would like to try it out to get more information.

Short Mood and Feelings Questionnaire (SMFQ)

This form is about how your child might have been feeling or acting **recently**.

For each question, please tick how s/he has been feeling or acting **in the past two weeks**.

If a sentence was not true about your child, check NOT TRUE.

If a sentence was only sometimes true, check SOMETIMES.

If a sentence was true about your child most of the time, check TRUE.

Score the questionnaire as follows:

NOT TRUE = 0

SOMETIMES = 1

TRUE = 2

	Not true	Some-times	True
1. S/he felt miserable or unhappy			
2. S/he didn't enjoy anything at all			
3. S/he felt so tired that s/he just sat around and did nothing			
4. S/he was very restless			
5. S/he felt s/he was no good any more			
6. S/he cried a lot			
7. S/he found it hard to think properly and concentrate			
8. S/he hated him/herself			
9. S/he felt s/he was a bad person			
10. S/he felt lonely			
11. S/he thought nobody really loved him/her			
12. S/he thought s/he could never be as good as other kids			
13. S/he felt s/he did everything wrong			

Short Mood and Feelings Questionnaire (SMFQ); Angold & Costello, 1987

First questionnaire score_____Date_____

Second score_____Date_____

Third score _____ Date _____

Fourth score_____Date_____

How clinical depression is diagnosed by clinicians

Depression in the healthcare setting can be referred to in a number of ways including; 'major depression', 'depressive illness', 'major depressive disorder', 'clinical depression' or 'unipolar depression'. A distinction is made between depression and other types of depressive illnesses such as 'dysthymia', 'bi-polar disorder' and 'psychotic depression'. This book will focus on the most common form of depressive illness in young people. There is information at the back of the book if you would like to find out more about other types of depressive illnesses.

Clinicians and doctors currently agree that in order for a young person to be diagnosed with depression they need to have several of the symptoms of depression for a period of at least two weeks and nearly every day. For a young person to 'meet criteria' fully, they need to be experiencing at least one core symptom and four or more further symptoms. There also needs to be significant impairment or distress as a result of the symptoms. There are some small variations in the criteria depending on which diagnostic guidelines are being followed (the most common one is the *Diagnostic and Statistical Manual of Mental Disorders*, 5th edition, or DSM-5). The severity of the depression will depend on how many symptoms the young person experiences and how much it is impacting on their life.

Depression is considered 'subclinical' if there are fewer than five symptoms and usually this means that a diagnosis of depression would not be given at that point. It may be that the young person is experiencing a smaller number of depression symptoms and these are interfering in their everyday life to some extent. This should not be ignored, however, because some young people, if they do not receive support at this point, may go on to develop other symptoms and their depression may get worse.

Depression may be categorised by professionals as MILD, MODERATE and SEVERE, depending on the number of symptoms present and the extent to which the symptoms interfere with the young person's normal functioning.

Sometimes symptoms may not be what they seem

The thing to look out for is that some of the symptoms of depression may not be immediately obvious and may actually be masquerading as something else. You may need to become a bit of a detective in order to notice these more *silent* signs. Below is a list of possible behaviours that could indicate symptoms of depression:

Other things to look out for

Frequent boredom, apparent 'laziness' or lack of interest in activities

Stubbornness, oppositional behaviour

Avoidance of situations/people

Sudden drop in marks or getting into trouble at school

Sleeping in really late, looking drowsy during the day, yawning a lot

Irritability, argumentativeness

Answering back or being overly negative

Lack of understanding or lack of sensitivity towards others

Being overly sensitive to things

Tantrums, outbursts of rage

Inability to start anything

Not wanting to eat with the family, moving food around the plate

Eating a lot of junk food

Being secretive, hiding away

Using drugs or alcohol

Often complaining of physical symptoms

Being overly quiet, detached

Not taking care of appearance and hygiene

Wearing long-sleeved clothing (to cover up self-harm scars)

Not getting things done, missing deadlines

But isn't some of this just normal teenage behaviour?

Of course many of the symptoms described above could be a normal picture of a teenager. Being a teenager can be hard work and there are many things for him or her to deal with, including relationships, school and exam pressures, changes in hormones and body shape, making decisions about the future and figuring out who they are! All these challenges do take their toll on teenagers and it is common to see mood changes and changes in behaviour. For example, sleeping patterns become unusual (how on earth can they sleep until lunchtime?!), arguments are much more likely as teenagers assert their independence, and you begin to feel as though you are running a hotel and taxi service as they spend more time on the computer or phone and less time with the family and in the house.

When looking at possible symptoms of depression it is helpful to compare them to what you know your child is normally like. This is not easy at all because as children move into adolescence, their behaviours can change dramatically anyway and at times parents feel like they are living with a stranger. Keep a close eye on things and make a note of what you observe and how often it's coming up. Pretty soon you will be able to tell the difference between 'teenage behaviour' and someone who is unhappy and withdrawn a lot of the time. The picture may also become a little clearer when you start to notice a cluster of symptoms that are significantly different to your child's usual personality and you notice that the symptoms are causing significant distress for your child or are interfering significantly in his or her life. Symptoms such as low mood and sadness or loss of interest in most activities that do not improve after a couple of weeks or more are unlikely to be simply explained by 'normal' teenage experience.

What you could do now

If you either suspect that your child has depression or you know this already the next best thing to do is to talk to them about your concerns. You may have done this already, or you may be apprehensive about doing this. There are times when it's difficult to talk to your teenager about various things but talking about possible depression is very important. It's definitely worth a go and the worst thing that may happen is they will just tell you to go away and leave them alone.

Parent reflections:

'As a parent what should I do? Your job as a parent is firstly to notice what is going on. You must become an observer of young people. 'Normal' teenage behaviour is so similar to the behaviour of depressed people that depression is hard to spot. When my son began to sleep a lot, didn't wash much, didn't communicate

---

and lived in a room that was a tip, that was normal, wasn't it? Because of my previous experience I was aware that I had to keep a subtle eye on him. When he began to express feelings of persistent low self-worth my alarm bells rang. When I realized he had stopped going out, not as he said because 'it was boring' but because he could not find the energy to get washed and dressed, we went to the GP and got an immediate referral to Child and Adolescent Mental Health Services (CAMHS).'

Ideas for conversations

Start out gently and use open-ended questions. It's best to keep questions simple. Write the questions down beforehand if this will help you to focus while having the conversation. Choose a time to talk when both you and your child are relatively calm.

For example:

'I've noticed that you're finding school (or other area) difficult lately, how are you feeling about it?'

'Have you been feeling really frustrated and upset with things lately?'

'I've noticed that you seem sad a lot of the time. Is that how you've been feeling?'

'You seem to spending a lot of time on your own lately and I was wondering whether there are things that are bothering you?'

'Are you still enjoying _____ (name usual hobbies or activities) or does it seem like an effort lately?'

'Do you feel sad/angry more times than you feel good?'

Take everything your child tells you seriously, even if it doesn't immediately make sense to you or you hear some things that are quite surprising or contrary to what you have observed. STAY CALM and be prepared to come back to these conversations regularly as your child may need some time to open up about his or her feelings. Although it is tempting, try not to be overly positive about what they are telling you and don't try to talk them out of how they are feeling. Show your child that you are patient, calm and available to support him or her, no matter what the problems may be.

If you think your child may be self-harming or is at risk of suicide, act immediately. See Chapter 3 on Safety now. Parents sometimes worry about asking questions about these issues but it is very important to ask your son or daughter so that you know how to support them in the best way.

If you are concerned that your child has depression we strongly urge you to now seek additional help and support from your GP. Depression can sometimes look like other medical problems (e.g. thyroid disorders), or it can be associated with other difficulties (e.g. substance abuse), therefore it is very important to seek professional assessment and advice. We have provided a brief summary of how to talk to your GP below.

A note about anxiety disorders

Depression in young people is often seen alongside anxiety disorders. It may be helpful for you to reflect on whether your child is also experiencing an anxiety problem. Some of the main anxiety problems that young people experience are listed below:

Generalized anxiety disorder (GAD) – excessive worrying about a range of things (for more than half the time) that is difficult to stop, along with physiological symptoms (e.g. difficulty falling asleep, aches and pains, irritability, tiredness, concentration difficulties).

Social phobia – fears about doing something embarrassing or being negatively judged by others in various social situations. Social situations are avoided or the person endures them with great distress. This is more than simple 'shyness', which a child can usually overcome with encouragement from other people.

Specific phobias – fears about specific situations or objects (e.g. spiders, heights, flying, injections, vomit, bees) that lead to avoidance or significant distress.

Panic disorder – extreme anxiety symptoms (e.g. fast heartbeat, breathlessness, dizziness, feelings of unreality, shaking, pins and needles) that seem to come out of the blue. The young person worries about having further panic attacks and this may restrict where he or she goes (see agoraphobia below).

Agoraphobia – intense fear of any situation where escape may be difficult or help may not be available (e.g. crowds, confined places, bridges, open places). Fears may be related to anxiety about the onset of a panic attack in these situations.

Obsessive Compulsive Disorder (OCD) – repetitive and intrusive thoughts or images that are distressing and unwanted (*obsessions*) together with compulsions to respond in a certain way (e.g. excessive washing, repetitive behaviour or rituals, checking) to these intrusive thoughts (in order to reduce the distress). People may experience a range of intrusive thoughts including thoughts about germs and contamination, harm coming to self or family, or things having to be a particular way (e.g. symmetry).

Post-Traumatic Stress Disorder (PTSD) – intense anxiety symptoms following a traumatic event where the person experiences or observes threat of death or harm to self or another person. The three main symptoms of PTSD are avoidance of reminders of the event, increased anxiety or hyperarousal and recurrent thoughts and/or images (flashbacks) or dreams about the event.

Separation Anxiety – this anxiety problem is more often seen in younger children but can also come up for teenagers. The anxiety is about harm coming to the child or their parent/carer/significant other when they are not together. The young person tries to avoid situations where they will be separated from their carer.

There is some significant overlap between anxiety and depression symptoms and we suggest you seek the guidance of a qualified professional to make the correct assessment (see below). Sometimes anxiety problems seem to be more severe

21

than low mood and 'cover up' the depression. This depends very much on how these problems are impacting on a young person's life. For example, a young person who has significant social anxiety may find it difficult to attend school, parties, or other social gatherings and to make any new friends. The impact of this will be felt on a daily basis, especially if the young person doesn't have the tools to deal with their anxiety symptoms. It may be likely that this young person also has low mood since their confidence and independence may be negatively affected by their anxiety. In this example it is likely that if the young person reduces their social anxiety, this may also have a positive impact on their low mood. Sometimes addressing the anxiety doesn't solve the depression and further work needs to be done to help the young person with their mood. Other times the depression needs attention first because it is severely affecting what the young person can do. When trying to figure out what to work on first it is best to identify together with a qualified professional which problem is causing the biggest impact or is most distressing for your child on a daily basis, and work on that first.

If you would find it helpful to write down your child's mood summary we have included a space for you to do this opposite:

My child's mood summary

Symptoms observed

Symptoms reported by my child

How long have symptoms been around for (more than two weeks)?

How often are the symptoms coming up (almost every day)?

Any obvious things that make it worse

Ways in which symptoms are interfering (at school, with friends, at home)

Any concerning behaviours or thoughts (e.g. risky behaviours or suicidal thoughts)

Things that seem to help

Treatment

Medication for depression

Medication is not usually the first type of treatment that is recommended for depression in young people. The National Institute of Clinical Excellence (NICE) is an organization in the UK that thoroughly evaluates the most effective treatments, based on high-quality research, for all health and mental health problems. These treatments are then recommended for use in the NHS. The current NICE recommendations for young people with depression state that talking therapies, or a combination of talking therapies and medication, should be provided.

Some parents are concerned about their children taking medication for their depressed mood and they are reluctant to try this approach. For young people with depression, only one anti-depressant is recommended. This is fluoxetine (Prozac). Fluoxetine is one of a group of drugs called selective serotonin reuptake inhibitors (SSRIs). These are believed to help by increasing the amount of serotonin (a neurotransmitter) that is available in the body and brain. Serotonin is thought to have a mood-boosting and anti-anxiety effect. It can be very difficult for some very depressed young people to make use of weekly talking therapy if they are experiencing severe symptoms such as concentration difficulties, very low energy or sleeping problems. For these young people, taking anti-depressants helps with some of these key symptoms, which may then make it easier for them to benefit more from the talking therapy. Some people report significant improvements from taking anti-depressants.

If you and your child do decide that taking anti-depressants is worth a try, please be aware that the benefits may not be felt for up to four weeks. It takes a bit of time for the medication to start to work so it's worth explaining this to your child in order to keep their expectations realistic. There may also be some side effects in the beginning, but usually these subside after a few days or weeks. If your child is eighteen years old or under, anti-depressants will not usually be prescribed by your GP. Your child will be referred to the local Child and Adolescent Mental Health Service (CAMHS), where the medication will be overseen by a specialist child and adolescent psychiatrist. They will review your son or daughter regularly and monitor their progress. It is important not to stop taking the anti-depressants before discussing this with your child's psychiatrist.

Talking therapies

There are several talking therapies that have been shown to be effective for young people with depression. These include Cognitive Behaviour Therapy (CBT), family therapy, Interpersonal Therapy (IPT) and psychodynamic psychotherapy. There are other approaches that are used in various settings but these haven't been researched as much for their effectiveness and the research evidence we have so far indicates that CBT is one of the most effective approaches for this type of problem (and for anxiety disorders). The availability of this treatment may depend on the services in your area and it is a good idea to ask your GP about this. The strategies in this book are based on CBT and we discuss the principles of CBT in more detail in chapter 6.

Talking to your GP

It's important to speak with your family GP as soon as possible if you suspect (or know) that your child is depressed. Ideally, this would be with your child's knowledge and agreement and we suggest you both go to the appointment.

When preparing for the appointment, keep the following things in mind:

- Make a double appointment so that you have enough time to discuss your concerns and to ask any questions
- Make a list of symptoms (together with your child, if possible) that you have noticed/observed and how long these have been present
- Think about any event or circumstances that may have contributed to the depression
- Feel free to take along the summary of your child's symptoms from this chapter and/or the questionnaire answers
- Help your child to prepare a list of any questions he or she may have and/or prepare a list of your own questions
- Let the GP know if there are any other family members who have depression now or had in the past
- If medication is discussed, make sure you get information about how long the medication takes to start working and any side effects to be aware of
- Your GP may initially suggest 'watchful waiting' in order to assess the severity of the depression. He or she may suggest a follow-up appointment a couple of weeks later before deciding on the best treatment plan

- Do ask questions about available talking therapies in your area and whether the GP is aware of waiting times
- Ask whether the GP will be referring your child to a local Child and Adolescent Mental Health Service (CAMHS) – this service would be able to provide your child (if under eighteen years) with a talking therapy and input from a psychiatrist regarding medication and safety, if relevant
- Don't be alarmed if the GP directly asks your child whether he or she has had thoughts about suicide or has attempted to hurt themselves – this is a frequent question asked so that the right support is put in place
- Mention any concerns you have about your child's risky or impulsive behaviours
- Make sure you are clear about what the next step is and whether any follow-up appointments are recommended with the GP
- There are no 'silly' questions when it comes to finding out more about depression and available support so feel free to ask anything that comes to mind

Other services and support

You may want to access other forms of support while waiting for your child to start treatment. Helping your child by following the suggestions in this book may be very useful at this point. We have put together a list of organizations, websites and other forms of support at the end of this book. This includes alternative places to look for treatment and organizations that can provide further advice.

Will my child get better?

Naturally, parents worry about the consequences of their child having depression. It is true that depression can be associated with other difficulties such as underachievement at school, social difficulties, substance abuse and other mental health difficulties. It is something that needs to be taken seriously but it isn't all bad news. Some young people who experience depression will get better on their own, without needing any additional help or treatment. What we know from studies is that a proportion of these young people will go on to develop depression again later in life if they don't receive the right treatment. Sometimes these relapses can happen within months of recovering from the first episode of depression. This suggests that treatment should be offered to all young people who are depressed for longer than several weeks. It's useful to bear in mind that having depression once doesn't mean that the young person will have it throughout their life, especially if they receive the right support. The good news is that many young people can overcome depression with the right treatment and support and they can go on to live their lives to the full.

Troubleshooting

What if my son or daughter refuses to talk to me/see the GP/other professional?

Obviously ideally it would be best for your child to see the GP or other professional with you but if he or she is refusing it would be a good idea for you to go to the appointment on your own anyway. This will help you to feel more supported and you can gather some information to feed back to your child, if possible.

It might also be helpful to find a compromise and encourage your child to face the situation gradually:

- I will go into the appointment but I'd like you to come in the car or stay in the waiting area

- Or, I will go to the first appointment and let you know what we said and then we go to the second appointment together

- Or, you can come for the first five/last five minutes of the appointment

- Or, I will do all of the talking and you can just listen if you want. I'll tell the doctor you're not ready to talk yet

Using this book

This book is for those parents or relatives who want to be more involved in a young person's recovery from depression. It may not be right for every family or for every young person with depression. You may find some strategies useful and others less so for your specific family and situation. This is fine, simply choose the things that feel right to you and don't feel pressure to apply everything. If the young person is receiving professional treatment it is not necessary to also follow guidelines in this book but it will complement treatment and may provide additional help.

Self-help

We believe that families and young people can make significant positive changes by using self-help materials such as those in this book. It is true that guidance by a therapist or other professional will often enable clients to make good progress and will help them to feel understood and less alone. Ultimately, however, even for those people in weekly treatment sessions, the changes that need to be made are up to them. There is no magic pill or formula that is given by the therapist to the young person or family (unfortunately)! The work is up to the young person with the family's support and progress is usually closely related to how much the young person has been able to apply the strategies between their sessions.

The strategies and principles in this book are based on CBT, as well as some additional strategies and ideas that have been found to be helpful for some young people and families in clinical practice. You can use this book on its own or alongside additional treatment that you and your child may be receiving. If it is the latter then please let the professionals you are working with know that you are following the advice in the book so that they are aware of the approaches you are trying out.

What order to follow?

Of course we think that it would be best if you followed the order as it is presented in this book but some people prefer to skip through things or pick the areas to work on first that seem the most relevant. This is fine. There is no right or wrong order when applying the strategies in this book but there are a few recommendations for the best effects. We suggest that you first become familiar with depression symptoms and observe how these relate to your child's difficulties (here in Chapter 1). If you are concerned about your child's suicidal thoughts and/ or risky behaviours then it's vital you skip ahead to Chapter 3. Then it's best to set some goals (Chapter 2) before moving onto other chapters. If you would like to become more familiar with the CBT approach then it will be useful to have a look at Chapter 6. After this it is very much dependent on what difficulties your child is experiencing. For example, if your child has lost interest in things and seems to have withdrawn from usual activities then we suggest you dive into Chapter 7. If you want to start out slowly and only apply a few strategies to begin with then we suggest using Chapters 7, 8 and 9. These chapters outline the main CBT strategies that have been shown to be helpful for young people with depression.

Examples

Throughout the book we will refer to the three families that we introduce later in this chapter. The teenagers of these families can also be found in the companion book for teenagers. The parents in these families try different approaches and we give examples of things that they have found helpful. Hopefully you may be able to relate to some of the difficulties they are experiencing and perhaps use some of the ideas that worked for them.

Strategies

We have suggested a number of different strategies for you to try with your child. Some of these may seem relevant for you and some not so much. If you are not sure if they will be helpful it may be good to try them for a while and see how you get on. It is worth giving things a good run for several weeks before making this decision. We have provided templates of diaries and worksheets so that you can keep a record of the things that you are observing and strategies that you are using. Recording things in this way provides a more objective view of how things are progressing and also provides an invaluable record to look back on and compare with in the future when things have changed.

Further information, support and troubleshooting

In some sections we have provided troubleshooting boxes with ideas and suggestions for the most common obstacles encountered by parents. In Appendix 1, on page 331, we have compiled a list of organizations, websites, books and places to find further information and support. Please have a look at this list now and perhaps mark the items that seem relevant to your current situation.

Your availability to your child

One of the most helpful and powerful things that parents can do is to be available to their child in various ways while their child is working on overcoming depression. This might sound very simple and very probably something that you are already doing. Please know that it is of immense value. The feedback from young people with depression time and time again indicates how good it is to know that their parents are there for them to talk to if and when they need it (even though they rarely tell their parents this or show it in their behaviour). The degree of availability that is needed and appropriate will vary greatly for each young person. For some it may simply mean knowing that they can talk and their parents will simply just listen. For others it is knowing they can start a conversation at any time with their parents about depression, or how they feel, and perhaps discuss the strategies they may be trying, without getting them too involved in the details. For some teenagers it may mean setting aside regular time when they can work with their parent(s) on strategies and make plans for further work. Yet for others it may mean having their parents become very involved for a period of time (e.g. when the depression is severe and significant support or monitoring is needed) and then stepping back and giving the young person more independence when they start to feel better.

Meet the parents of Robert, Lin and Emily

Hayley – Robert's mum

I have two children, Robert, who is nearly eighteen, and Rebecca, who is twenty-two. Life is not easy as I have to work hard to make ends meet and I have very little time for anything else. I have two jobs. I work as a dinner lady and in the evenings I do a cleaning job. Robert and Rebecca's dad left a few years back and although I'm now over the divorce and the whole thing, it's still pretty hard being on my own and knowing that he has another wife and family. I'm lucky that my kids are still at home but this sometimes has its own problems. Robert and Rebecca are just not getting along at all lately. They argue all the time and I'm always being pulled into their arguments. Come to think of it, Robert has been really snappy and argumentative for a while now, and not just with Rebecca. Everything I say to him seems to be the wrong thing and we often end up having shouting matches or he'll just storm off to his room. He stays there for hours. I'm really not sure what he's doing in there and it's such a complete mess I just don't go in there anymore. It's usually covered with empty crisp and chocolate packets and no wonder he doesn't seem to want to eat his dinners. He seems to be spending a lot of time on his own because he's not seeing his friends very often and not playing football like he used to. It must be a phase he's going through, probably a teenage thing, but I don't remember Rebecca being like this when she was younger. Perhaps it's what boys are like. He's been getting into trouble at school as well and this worries me a lot because I want him to finish school and get a good job. Hopefully he'll snap out of it soon. It's really not easy being a single mum and although the kids are nearly adults, they still need feeding and a roof over their heads. At times my life gets me down but there's no time or use crying over things you can't change.

Things that Robert's mum wasn't aware of:

Robert had been feeling worse and worse about a number of things for quite a while. He hadn't been picked for a new football team and this was a big disappointment to him because football was a big part of his life. He didn't want to burden his mum about it so he kept it to himself. Robert had also broken up with his girlfriend, which his mum did know about, but he hadn't told her how much he still missed her and how upset he was about it, especially as now she was going out with one of his friends. Robert was having some problems with his friendships as well, and school was not going well because he found it really hard to care about the work and to focus in class. Robert was getting into arguments and fights at school and the teachers had told his mum about this. Robert's mum tried to regularly encourage Robert to do well and to try as hard as he could but this often led to arguments at home. Despite his mum's efforts, Robert felt very alone and just wanted to shut the whole world out. He didn't feel like eating anything and sometimes thought about wanting it all to end.

Robert's possible signs of depression that Hayley has noticed:

Snappy and argumentative

Stays in his room

Not eating dinners

Not seeing friends

Not playing football

Getting into trouble at school

Robert's possible signs of depression that Hayley wasn't aware of:

Upset about girlfriend and about not being picked for the football team

Can't focus in class

Doesn't care about school

Feeling alone and wanting to be alone

Thoughts about wanting it all to end

Sue and Lee – Lin's mum and dad

We are from Hong Kong and we've lived in the UK for about ten years. We have moved around the UK quite a bit, mainly due to Lee's work, but we are hoping this recent move is our last for a while. We have three children, our eldest, Kim, is twenty-one and we are so proud that she is studying to become a medical doctor. It was hard when she had to move out of home to go to university but we are used to it now and she seems to be coping fine. Lin, our second daughter, is sixteen and we have a son, Sam, who is nearly eleven. Sam is a bright boy and he loves his new school. He can be a bit mischievous at times but generally he is a good boy. Lin is also very intelligent; we hope she follows in her sister's footsteps and chooses a good career for her future. Lin is being a typical teenager lately. She seems so moody all the time and she's always sleeping. It's also such an effort to get her to join in anything and she's been forgetting to do her chores. She's not doing the things she used to such as shopping, doing arty things and seeing friends. She has not been applying herself to her schoolwork and homework and this concerns us, as we want her to do well and get good marks so she can get into a good university. She says she doesn't like the school and people there. We find it hard to talk to her about it because she gets upset very easily and then just avoids us and stays in her room. This is very hard on Lin's mother, Sue, because she has been feeling quite sad lately and the doctor even suggested she might be depressed. He has prescribed some medication but we think this is not necessary and it should pass once we are more settled in this new area. Hopefully Lin will also settle down soon and start seeing more sense. We did wonder whether she might be feeling quite sad too, especially as she had to leave her friends and school not that long ago.

Things that Lin's parents were not aware of:

Lin was finding the most recent family move very difficult. She had made some good friends at her old school and she was really missing them, especially her best friend Amy. Lin didn't feel she could fit in with any group at school and she was convinced that others were talking about her behind her back. She was also convinced that she would be the only one that wasn't invited to a big summer party. At school Lin was finding it hard to concentrate on her work and she was worried that her usually high marks would get worse. She would eat lunch on her own or stay in the library so that others wouldn't look at her. Lin felt tired most of the time and tried to sleep as much as possible so that she didn't have to think so much and so that she could feel less tired. She felt 'no good at anything' and found it incredibly difficult to do any of the things that she previously enjoyed. Sometimes Lin has thoughts about never having been born.

Lin's possible signs of depression that her parents have noticed:

Moody all the time

Always sleeping

Not joining in things

Forgetful

Not doing schoolwork

Becomes easily upset

Spends time alone

Lin's possible signs of depression that her parents were not aware of:

Lots of negative thoughts and predictions

Difficulties with concentration

Very tired

Feeling 'no good'

Not engaging in activities

Thoughts about not being born

Fiona and Chris – Emily's mum and stepdad

We met when we both already had children from other relationships and we have been together for about eight years now. We have two children who live with us, Emily, who is fourteen, and William, who is twelve. They are Fiona's children. Chris's children live with his ex. We are very lucky to have much of our family living close by. We are always meeting up and doing things together and there's always someone to help out with the kids or other things. The kids are very upset at the moment because our beloved dog, Charlie, had to be put down. It's so hard to prepare your children for things like this. It seems to have hit Emily the hardest and we think she misses him a lot. Emily has been so quiet the past few months and we have noticed this at family events too.

She used to love going to see her cousins but now we have to drag her there. We also have to work really hard to get her to go to school. She is often complaining about feeling sick, or having a headache, and she begs us to let her stay home from school. Sometimes it's hard to know what to do. We took her to see the GP to see what was going on but they couldn't find anything wrong, thankfully. So now we just tell her to try her best and we encourage her to go to school each morning, but it's obvious she is finding this very hard. The teachers have mentioned that she has been crying at school. We thought this was probably to do with Charlie dying but now we are wondering what else might be going on.

Things that Fiona and Chris weren't aware of:

Emily doesn't like going to school because she is being bullied by some girls who she wants to be friends with. This started a few months ago and the girls catch the same school bus as Emily and sometimes give her a hard time. Emily has been crying at school but she hasn't told the teachers or the school nurse about the bullies. Emily wants to be accepted by this group of girls and she doesn't want to get them into trouble. Emily is feeling very tired and unhappy most of the time. She experiences a lot of physical symptoms as well. Emily has lost all interest in seeing her family and doing family activities; it feels like too much effort to her.

Emily's possible signs of depression that Fiona and Chris have noticed:

Unusually quiet

Doesn't want to go to family activities

Wants to avoid school

Complains of physical symptoms

Crying at school

Emily's possible signs of depression that Fiona and Chris weren't aware of:

Feeling tired and unhappy

Being bullied at school

Things seem like too much of an effort

We will return to the parents of Robert, Lin and Emily later in the book.

2

Setting goals

Parent reflections:

'So first you've tried to watch out [for the depression symptoms]!
Then when you've spotted it and had that difficult first conversation with your child, you have to realize what has taken place.
Together, you have both taken the difficult first step to getting
better. You need to be aware of that pivotal first moment and
you need to be aware that you are setting out together to go on
a journey of discovery without knowing the destination.'

Setting goals might seem an obvious thing to do but many
people don't usually do this in a clear and structured way.
This means that goals tend to stay vague and general. So, for
example, many parents reading this book may have goals
for their children or for themselves such as 'for my child to
be happy', 'for my child to do well in school and beyond', 'to
help my child overcome depression', 'for my child to be more
confident or have a higher self-esteem', 'to spend more time
as a family'. While having general goals is an excellent start,
breaking them down into specific and clear targets helps to

move things in the right direction more quickly. It also makes it easier to measure whether things are improving. It's been found time and time again that setting these smaller, relevant and more measurable goals helps people to be more motivated towards achieving them. In order to keep motivated, the goals also need to feel achievable. Sometimes breaking goals down into short-, medium- and long-term timeframes can also be a helpful strategy.

It might be tempting to skip over this section but it's well worth the effort spending a little bit of time thinking about your goals. You may find that you need to come back to this section once you have read a few later chapters about what helps with depression. You may want to set goals for your child, for yourself and even for the whole family.

In the example below, you will notice that there are many 'doing' ideas for goals and you may be wondering what these have in common with getting over depression or feeling better about yourself in general. We go into this in much more detail in Chapter 7 and we also talk about life values in relation to activities. In short, doing more, being with others and becoming more involved in life's small details can have a significant positive impact on mood, especially when you start adding up all the small activities and achievements. It might not seem like a big enough leap towards overcoming depression for a young person to begin to help with dinner or to see a friend once a week. However, these very small steps are important. With persistence and patience having a range of small goals such as this can start to make a difference. The small goals begin to give the young person a sense of achievement and belonging and pretty soon more and more goals can be added. We know the big picture and destination is overcoming depression and feeling good. We assure you that taking it one small goal and step at a time with patience and perseverance is an effective way of getting to this destination.

Let's go through an example and let's start with the big picture:

First, it might be a good idea to write a 'problem list' related to the depression. Once you have a list of the main problems it is then easier to match these up with specific goals.

Problem List:

Moody/low most days

Not doing much

Keeping away from people

Not interested in activities

Long-term goal:

I want my child to be less low/happier

Now let's look at the more immediate future:

What would my child be doing (or not doing) this week or next if he or she were feeling less depressed?

Here are some prompts to help you think about different situations:

With the family:

e.g. watching television together with the family, taking the dog for a walk with me, joining in family BBQ or other family gathering, spending more time downstairs/with family in the kitchen, going shopping or to dinner together.

With friends:

e.g. having a friend over to the house after school, meeting up with friends at the weekend, staying at a friend's house over-night or going there for dinner, arranging activities with friends.

At school:

e.g. completing homework on time rather than leaving it until the last minute, attending school regularly, talking to me about school subjects and upcoming assignments, talking to teachers about any difficulties, joining in with school activities and sports.

On their own:

e.g. doing the things they used to like to do such as reading, lifting weights, watching favourite films, looking after their appearance, running, looking at magazines, arranging personal appointments, getting a haircut, organizing paperwork or documents, going to bed at regular times.

In the morning:

e.g. getting up at a regular time each day, preparing and eating breakfast, having a shower, having a conversation with me before school, helping out with the morning chores, taking the dog out, feeding the pets.

In the evening:

e.g. doing some exercise, joining the family for dinner, helping out with food preparation, getting clothes and books ready for school, spending less time in his or her room, phoning a friend or relative, playing a game on the computer with us.

During the weekends:

e.g. going swimming, joining a club, helping out around the house and garden, doing some volunteering or a part-time job, seeing friends or relatives, joining in family fun activities, doing homework, spending time on hobbies, going out shopping with friends, having boyfriend/girlfriend over.

During the week:

e.g. going to school every day on time, catching the bus on his or her own, attending after-school clubs or activities, just relaxing with the family after homework, spending quality time in her or his room on relaxing or absorbing activities, helping out with clearing up after dinner.

Hopefully you've managed to think of some specific goals based on what you would like to see your child doing more of.

Now it's time to check this out with your child. It's all very well coming up with some great goals but if your child doesn't agree with these then they are not likely to happen! It's best to do this gently and with a good rationale for the suggestions, otherwise the young person may feel criticized that they are not doing enough. People with depression often interpret many things in a negative way and are much more likely to hear well-meaning things in a critical way (more on this in a later chapter). It's usually best to start with something positive you have noticed that your child is doing already, and building on this. Of course your child may already have some ideas and be motivated to work towards some goals of their own, so it's worth checking this first and then working together to form a plan based on their goals first.

Lin's mum, Sue, approached the topic in the following way:

Sue picked an evening when she could see that Lin was in a better mood and more relaxed to talk to her about setting some goals for overcoming low mood. Sue was aware that Lin was cutting herself off from her friends and family and spending a lot of time alone. This was one of the problems that Sue listed on the 'problem list'. Sue mentioned to Lin that she had noticed that when Lin spoke to her friends on the phone or when she saw them at the weekend this seemed to lift her mood, sometimes for several hours. Lin agreed that sometimes it was OK. Sue told Lin she had read that overcoming depression involves doing more of the things that seem to lift mood, even if it's hard sometimes, and even when you don't feel like doing it at first. She wondered whether Lin would like to keep in contact with friends more regularly. Lin said that she sometimes wasn't in the mood so this would put pressure on her. Sue agreed that putting pressure on Lin wouldn't be a good idea so she asked how often would feel OK for her over the next couple of weeks. Lin suggested she contacts her friends two times in the week to begin with, once on the phone and maybe once via text to arrange to meet up. Sue agreed and said this was a great start. She asked Lin if it would be OK if she reminded her of this every couple of days and Lin said that was fine as long as she didn't nag her. They wrote down the goal on a piece of paper and put this next to the phone in the hallway. They agreed to check at the end of each week to see if it was being achieved and helping Lin feel better or not. Lin seemed pleased by this plan and by the fact that her mum wanted to think about it with her so Sue decided to mention another goal of getting involved in cooking and baking more, something which Lin used to like doing quite a lot.

As in the example above, it's a good idea to regularly review whether the goal is being reached (you can use a simple scale from 0 – not made any moves towards the goal, to 10 – reached the goal completely). It's also helpful to review whether this is making a difference to how your child is feeling.

As you're working on goals with your child sometimes you will both realize that the goal needs to change (for example, it needs to be smaller or bigger) or new goals need to be established. It's an ongoing process of monitoring and reviewing and it can often be worth the effort.

Troubleshooting

What if my son or daughter doesn't want to work on any of the goals that I have set?

It's best to work on something that motivates your child so a good start is to begin with your child's goals, even if they don't seem like the most relevant ones to begin with. Once your child has made progress on their own goals you can gradually introduce your ideas as well.

There is often some overlap between a parent's and child's goals so see if you can find the middle ground (e.g. parent wants their daughter to spend less time hiding away in her room. Young person wants to see friends more often. The two goals overlap to a large degree).

My child's problem list

My child's agreed goals

Long-term goals

Medium-term goals

Short-term goals

Progress chart

Weeks 1/2

Goal 1 _____ Progress   0 1 2 3 4 5 6 7 8 9 10
(0 = no progress at all, 10 = completely reached my goal)

Goal 2 _____ Progress   0 1 2 3 4 5 6 7 8 9 10
(0 = no progress at all, 10 = completely reached my goal)

Goal 3 _____ Progress   0 1 2 3 4 5 6 7 8 9 10
(0 = no progress at all, 10 = completely reached my goal)

Weeks 3/4

Goal 1 _____ Progress   0 1 2 3 4 5 6 7 8 9 10
(0 = no progress at all, 10 = completely reached my goal)

Goal 2 _____ Progress   0 1 2 3 4 5 6 7 8 9 10
(0 = no progress at all, 10 = completely reached my goal)

Goal 3 _____ Progress   0 1 2 3 4 5 6 7 8 9 10
(0 = no progress at all, 10 = completely reached my goal)

Weeks 5/6

Goal 1 _____ Progress   0 1 2 3 4 5 6 7 8 9 10
(0 = no progress at all, 10 = completely reached my goal)

Goal 2 _____ Progress   0 1 2 3 4 5 6 7 8 9 10
(0 = no progress at all, 10 = completely reached my goal)

Goal 3 _____ Progress   0 1 2 3 4 5 6 7 8 9 10
(0 = no progress at all, 10 = completely reached my goal)

Weeks 7/8

Goal 1 _____ Progress   0 1 2 3 4 5 6 7 8 9 10
(0 = no progress at all, 10 = completely reached my goal)

Goal 2 _____ Progress   0 1 2 3 4 5 6 7 8 9 10
(0 = no progress at all, 10 = completely reached my goal)

Goal 3 _____ Progress   0 1 2 3 4 5 6 7 8 9 10
(0 = no progress at all, 10 = completely reached my goal)

Weeks 9/10

Goal 1 _____ Progress   0 1 2 3 4 5 6 7 8 9 10
(0 = no progress at all, 10 = completely reached my goal)

Goal 2 _____ Progress   0 1 2 3 4 5 6 7 8 9 10
(0 = no progress at all, 10 = completely reached my goal)

Goal 3 _____ Progress   0 1 2 3 4 5 6 7 8 9 10
(0 = no progress at all, 10 = completely reached my goal)

Weeks 11/12

Goal 1 _____ Progress   0 1 2 3 4 5 6 7 8 9 10
(0 = no progress at all, 10 = completely reached my goal)

Goal 2 _____ Progress   0 1 2 3 4 5 6 7 8 9 10
(0 = no progress at all, 10 = completely reached my goal)

Goal 3 _____ Progress   0 1 2 3 4 5 6 7 8 9 10
(0 = no progress at all, 10 = completely reached my goal)

Part 2

Safety and
basic mood lifters

3

Safety

This chapter is for any parent who is concerned about their child's self-harming, risky behaviours and/or suicidal thoughts. Even if this is something that is not an issue for your child it is still worth reading through as this can sometimes be a taboo subject that isn't discussed enough. There may be some thoughts and ideas here that you haven't come across before so it's a good idea to check this for yourself. Many young people with depression experience thoughts about suicide and some young people respond to their feelings and thoughts by hurting themselves. These reactions are usually an attempt by the young person to try to cope with feelings and situations that they find overwhelming or hopeless. If we keep in mind that these are **coping strategies**, we can feel more hopeful about being able to help and make positive changes and introduce safer coping methods.

While suicide attempts and self-harm are extremely serious matters that require emergency attention, we also want to reassure parents that many young people with depression do not engage in these behaviours. Fleeting suicidal thoughts are common but a large proportion of young people do not go on

59

to hurt themselves significantly, particularly if they have some support mechanisms in place.

As highlighted in the introductory chapter, we encourage parents to ask specific questions about suicidal thoughts and risky behaviours such as self-harm or substance abuse. This can be very difficult and we recommend that you immediately seek the support of a professional with this. The fear that some parents have is that talking about it may put ideas into their child's mind. This is not what we have found in clinical practice. Our advice is that talking about it is necessary and often young people are very relieved when asked about their difficult thoughts. It may be something that they have been hiding and it may have felt very frightening to experience such thoughts. They may have been thinking that they are the only ones who think this way and there may be feelings of shame and guilt or that there may be something 'wrong' with them.

By opening up the subject and asking specific questions what you are also doing is giving your child the messages that

1. these types of thought are common in people with depression and nothing to be ashamed of

2. you are able to hear and handle anything they tell you (even though you may be feeling frightened inside about what they may say)

3. something can be done to help and you will be there to support them every step of the way

We have made some suggestions of questions to ask in case you are wondering where to start (but please seek professional help as well):

'I know you have been feeling down (or depressed, low, sad, blue, or whatever word feels right for your child) lately. When people are sad a lot of the time they can sometimes think more about death and dying or just not wanting to be around anymore. Have you been having thoughts like these?'

'From what I have read this happens to a lot of people. What sort of thoughts have you been having?'

'I've noticed you've often been upset. Do you ever feel like "what's the point anymore?" Do you ever think about hurting yourself in any way?'

'Have there been times when you just didn't care what happens, and perhaps you were really reckless or did things that could have hurt you and you didn't care?'

'Have you ever hurt yourself in any way?'

'Have you ever thought of a way to hurt yourself? Tell me more about it.'

If your child tells you about suicidal thoughts or urges it's important to strike a balance between taking it very seriously but not reacting with panic or other extreme emotions such as anger or distress. The main thing to convey is that you are very pleased that they have been able to tell you about this and together you will find a way to overcome it.

These are very tricky things to bring up and you may need to find your own words and ways of asking. If you are unable to bring this up with your child but you are quite concerned it might be a good idea to speak to their siblings or close friends to see if they know anything. Sometimes young people find it much easier to talk to their friends or other young people about these issues. If this doesn't help and you are still concerned then have a look at some of the resources and websites on pages 331–337 for further advice. It will be a good idea to schedule an appointment with your child to see the GP so that you can raise your concerns with the GP and he or she can help to assess the situation. Of course if your child is seeing someone for treatment then the therapist will be keeping an eye on these types of issues and will keep you informed about anything serious. If you suspect that your child is not talking about these issues openly with the therapist then let the therapist know about your concerns and ask him or her to assess this further.

Self-harm

Self-harm is a phrase that unfortunately we hear quite often when working with young people in mental health services. It refers to any harmful acts or behaviours that a young person directs towards themselves. This can include acts such as pinching skin, cutting arms, legs or torso with razors, scissors or other implements, hitting the body or the head against something, burning the skin with a cigarette, engaging in risky behaviour such as drug taking, drinking large amounts of alcohol, having unprotected sex, reckless driving or bike riding. While it is very concerning for parents when their child engages in self-harming behaviours, it is important to try to remain calm and to develop an understanding of the motivation and function of the behaviour.

The following list gives examples of reasons why some people self-harm:

- Feeling *something* rather than the usual numbness
- Feeling *anything else* rather than the distressing emotions
- Escaping from feelings of depression, fear, shame or guilt
- Escaping from distressing thoughts or images
- Relieving feelings of anger or frustration
- Punishing self or others
- Having control over something (when other things feel out of control)
- Taking feelings out on own body
- Letting others know how bad things really are
- Communicating something else to others
- Wanting more support but not knowing how else to ask for it
- Following and copying the behaviour of others in order to have a feeling of belonging

If your son or daughter self-harms, can you identify any of the reasons in this list? You may not know at this point, this is very common. The young person may not fully understand these behaviours yet either. Whatever the reason, it is usually a way of **coping** with something that feels difficult. Once these coping strategies are understood, we can begin to think about changing some of them into more helpful and less harmful coping strategies. This takes time and therefore everyone needs to be very patient with the young person. A young person who has been self-harming him or herself for a long time will rarely be able to stop these behaviours immediately. A gradual approach of reducing self-harm, introducing more helpful strategies, and reinforcing any positive changes (through praise, positive attention, encouragement or other meaningful reward strategies) will increase the chances of progress. Any setbacks need to also be approached with patience and understanding in order to help the young person to identify the triggers and work towards reducing the chances of the triggers in the future.

Have a look at the items listed below and if possible, discuss these with your child so that you both develop a better understanding.

Triggers to self-harm (what seems to set it off or make it more likely that your child self-harms?)

Main reasons for self-harm (how does it seem to help your child cope at the time, for example, to stop overwhelming feelings or to block things out?)

What seems to help (situations or people who seem to help your child to not self-harm)?

Safety planning

If you have been able to speak with your child and your child has revealed suicidal thoughts and/or self-harming behaviours it is important to put safety measures in place right away.

First, you will need to find out whether your child has actually thought of a way of hurting themselves. People who have thought of specific methods or who have made specific plans are more at risk. Find out as much detail as possible about this, while doing everything you can to remain calm, understanding and open-minded. Try to find out if your child has already attempted anything in the past.

- If the situation is urgent (e.g. your child is expressing the wish to die and he or she has specific plans to hurt themselves, or your child cannot reassure you that he or she will not hurt themselves, or your child has hurt themselves already) then please either call 111 or 999 for advice or go straight to your local A&E department. Many families don't realize that these services are available to help with these types of problem. There is usually an 'on-call psychiatrist' on duty at A&E departments who can provide the appropriate assessment, advice and support. Alternatively, speak to your GP straight away.
- If your child is already being seen in a Child and Adolescent Mental Health service then call the service straight away and discuss your concerns with the duty staff member.
- For less urgent situations it is best to make a GP appointment for you and your child as soon as possible so that a plan for treatment can be discussed and put in place.

- In the meantime it is a good idea for you and your child to make a list of things that may help them to stay safe – see suggestions in the **safety card or emergency toolkit** below.

- Become familiar with the support organizations in Appendix 1. The ones we have suggested have confidential telephone support lines and a wealth of information on their websites. Some have specific sections for parents and separate support material and telephone numbers for young people. Look these up NOW and make a list of the ones you like and their telephone numbers.

- Keep close observation of your child's behaviour and mood. Be on the lookout for any warning signs such as these:

  ◊ A sudden shift in mood either up or down (e.g. your child expressing a lot of hopelessness about many things or a sudden improvement in mood for no apparent reason – sometimes people who have decided to end their life suddenly feel better as if a weight has been lifted).

  ◊ Your child mentioning death, dying or funerals casually in conversations or joking about it.

  ◊ Any notes about it left lying around or on the computer.

  ◊ Substance use (e.g. alcohol or drugs).

  ◊ Any other unusual behaviour such as your child suddenly apologizing to others for things they may have done in the past or giving possessions away to others.

- Take precautions by removing and locking away all medicines and other things that may be harmful (e.g. razor blades). Of course you may not be able to keep all items away from your teenager but it is about minimizing the accessibility of these things, particularly as acts of self-harm are sometimes impulsive. Therefore not having items to hand can sometimes allow enough delay for the urges to subside. Ask your child whether they have anything that they have used to harm themselves with in the past. If your child tells you about any items, negotiate with them that for the time being you would like to keep these items away from them.
- Ask your child to talk to you regularly about these thoughts and agree together that if he or she feels worse or if these thoughts get stronger that they will talk to you straight away.
- Involve other members of the family when appropriate in order to support the young person.
- Avoid family arguments and conflict, if possible.

Prepare a card such as the one opposite with your child. Keep one copy in the house and ask your child to keep the other copy with them at all times (e.g. in a wallet). They can also input important telephone numbers in their mobile, if they have one.

My emergency toolkit

People your child will contact when having suicidal thoughts/urges to self-harm,

for example:

1. Mother and/or father: face to face or mobile numbers 00000 000000 and 00000 000000

2. Other relative, e.g. brother: mobile 00000 000000, landline 00000 000000

3. School nurse/teacher: face to face

4. GP: GP telephone number and out of hours number

5. Responsible friend: mobile 00000 000000

6. Support organizations or crisis phone numbers (e.g. ChildLine or Samaritans, see list on pages 331–337, note the telephone numbers down)

7. Nearest A&E department for on-call psychiatrist

Triggers that seem to make your child's mood worse or increase the likelihood of suicidal thoughts and/or urges to self-harm, for example:

1. Arguments with friends/family

2. Spending too much time on social media sites

3.   Spending too much time alone

4.   Substances (e.g. alcohol)

5.   Bullying or being in trouble with the law

List of useful distractions, for example:

1.   Watching a funny programme on television

2.   Helping with gardening or dinner

3.   Going for a jog/walk/to the gym/drawing

4.   Phoning someone

List of other coping strategies to prevent harm, for example:

1.   Writing feelings down

2.   Punching a pillow or screaming into the pillow

3.   Listening to uplifting music

4.   Flicking a rubber band against the skin, putting an ice cube on the skin or pinching (instead of cutting)

Robert's mum, Hayley, had been worried that since Robert seemed so depressed and hopeless, he may have been having thoughts about hurting himself in some way. Hayley found it so hard to know how to bring the subject up. She decided to write down three things to ask Robert and waited until he seemed to be in a calm mood to bring it up. Hayley first mentioned to Robert that she had noticed he had been really low lately. Robert grunted something back and didn't seem interested. Hayley then said that she was there if he wanted to talk about it any time. She then said that she wanted to help and she wanted to make sure he was OK. The subject was then dropped since Hayley noticed Robert didn't want to talk.

Several days later Hayley brought it up again. This time she said that she wanted Robert to tell her about any difficult thoughts that he may have been having. She said that many people sometimes have thoughts about wanting things to stop in some way and she wondered whether he had ever thought this. Robert said he didn't know what she was talking about and then walked out and to his room. Hayley felt a bit deflated but also relieved that she had at least put the subject 'out there'. To her surprise, the following day Robert asked if he could talk to her. He told her that he had been thinking those things lately and it scared him. Hayley told Robert that she was really glad he told her. She also said that many people have these sorts of thoughts when they feel bad. She remembered the three things she wanted to ask him, which included how often he thought this, whether he had any specific plans, and whether he had ever tried anything before to hurt himself.

This was not an easy conversation but both Robert and Hayley were very relieved to be having it. Hayley found out that Robert had been having thoughts about dying quite often, but that he hadn't done anything about them and he didn't have any plans to hurt himself. It was so good for Hayley to know about these things in detail. Hayley knew that Robert drank alcohol from time to time and she asked him not to do this while he was feeling so low. They agreed to make an appointment to speak with the GP to see if there was anything that could be done to help Robert feel better. Hayley asked Robert to promise her he would come to talk to her when the thoughts came up again. He agreed reluctantly. Hayley told Robert about a couple of the websites and support organizations and he said he might have a look at them later. They then drew up a safety card/emergency tool-kit for him to keep in his wallet. Robert also saved the emergency numbers on his mobile. After this Hayley suggested that rather than stay at home that evening perhaps they could go out to the cinema as a treat for both of them.

Troubleshooting

I really don't know whether my child is having these types of thought or whether s/he is hurting themselves in any way. It's too difficult to talk to him or her about it or s/he won't talk to me and I'm really worried.

We stress how important it is not to be facing this on your own. If your child will agree to see the GP with you then this is the place to bring up your concerns. If your child won't go to the appointment at this stage then we suggest you go to the appointment on your own or with your partner and discuss your concerns with the GP. In addition, have a look at the resources at the back of the book (e.g. Papyrus, Harmless, Young Minds)

4

Helping your child get 'back to basics'

In this book we want to help you use theories and research from psychology to help your child tackle low mood and overcome depression. Sometimes theories and research support simple common sense. In this chapter we want to remind you about some of the simple things that all parents can do to support and help their child. These simple things are likely to remind you of how you cared for your child when they were much younger. As they have grown older it's likely that you, like most other parents, have stood back and allowed your child to take over. However, when your child is older and is depressed it can be very helpful to offer them a bit of extra support and help. The kind of things we discuss in this chapter that can help improve your child's mood and wellbeing are:

- Sleeping
- Eating
- Taking exercise

It is likely that when your son or daughter was in primary

school you were mostly in charge of these things. You, or another adult, decided when your child went to bed, you woke them in the morning and decided on their mealtimes and also what they ate. You, or another adult, took them to school and collected them at the end of the day. You, or someone else, probably also took them to many of their out-of-school activities and classes. You and their school made sure that they had regular exercise.

As your child has become older and more independent it is natural that they have become more responsible for making decisions about their day-to-day life. They almost certainly go to bed much later than they did as a younger child. They may decide for themselves at what time to go to bed. Older teenagers may now stay up later than you do and not wake up until lunchtime at weekends. Young people with depression often have sleep patterns that are quite extreme. Outside of school hours most teenagers also have a lot more freedom to decide how to spend their time. Different families have different expectations about how much time they spend together, but in general, most teenagers spend more time alone or with their friends, and less time with their families as they get older.

It is right to give teenagers more responsibility as they learn how to become adults. They need to learn how to manage their own time. They need to find out what happens if they don't get enough sleep, or don't eat well. They need to discover how to organize their activities so that they can manage to get important things done but still have time for fun. When they are spending time with friends of their own age, teenagers need to learn how to handle disagreements, how to keep safe, and how to resist temptation and trouble.

Making mistakes and learning how to correct them is a very important part of moving towards independence. Most parents would prefer their teenage child to make mistakes while they are still living at home and have the support of their parents and other family members. However, it is still useful for parents to provide some structure to help their teenager to make good decisions and to avoid making big mistakes. Getting the balance between providing a structure that is supportive and flexible and standing back and allowing your teenage son or daughter to make their own mistakes is one of the greatest challenges that parents face. No parent finds this easy and all parents have times when they get it wrong. In this chapter our aim is to give you some pointers to help you and your family get the balance that is right for you.

The effects of depression on 'the basics'

Sleep problems and eating problems are some of the core symptoms of depression. Sleep problems can include not being able to get to sleep, waking early in the morning and not feeling refreshed, having sleep rhythms that are completely different to everyone else in the family, and sleeping for many, many hours. Eating problems often include not having any appetite and simply 'going off' food, but also include eating too much, eating too much junk food, and skipping family meals. The effects of poor sleep and poor diet add to other problems of depression including having trouble concentrating, thinking, planning and making judgments, and feeling exhausted and hopeless. These difficulties make it very hard to take part in normal activities at school, with friends and at home and many young people find themselves doing less and less when they are depressed.

These problems can create a vicious cycle with each problem making each of the others more difficult to manage. For most young people the changes that come along with depression are not things that they notice immediately – the changes happen gradually and creep up over time. Usually by the time the young person is aware that they feel low and sad they are already sleeping badly, eating badly and finding that they are doing less and less. As well as being hard to notice, young people who feel depressed and low usually have a very low opinion of themselves. They are likely to see themselves as useless or worthless. It can be hard to see the point of making an effort or to see that any change is possible.

You may have noticed similar changes in your son's or daughter's behaviour. It is incredibly difficult for them to keep doing normal activities if they feel low in mood. You may have noticed that they spend a lot more time in their room, on their own. They may have stopped doing things out of school, may not see their friends so much, and they may have fallen behind with schoolwork. Some young people who feel low in mood find other young people who feel the same. This may be helpful but spending a lot of time with other people who are depressed can also reinforce their own low mood, draw attention to problems, and encourage them to be more introspective and less active.

Figure 1 below shows how these problems are often linked together and form a vicious cycle. Typically, something bad or upsetting happens to the young person (a negative life event). This then makes it hard for them to carry on with their usual activities and this then in turn keeps their mood low and makes them feel even worse.

Figure 1

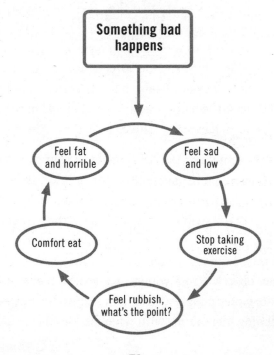

Remember Robert? He used to do a lot of things that kept him healthy without even noticing that he was doing them. His mum didn't ever need to worry about him keeping busy. He loved football and played at every opportunity. As well as making him feel good, playing football kept Robert physically fit, was a way to spend time with his friends, gave him an appetite so he ate well, and tired him out so he slept well at night.

How is Robert now?

- He doesn't play football any more – so he gets less exercise
- He eats a lot of junk food
- He spends a lot of time on his own
- He stays up late at night playing on his Xbox – he can't then wake up in the morning

These different behaviours have not made Robert depressed but they do make him feel worse and worse. They keep him depressed and feeling low.

For Robert, there were two different 'negative life events'. First, his girlfriend dumped him and started to go out with his friend. Second, he was dropped from the football team. These two events meant that he spent a lot more time alone, and this then exacerbated his feelings of low mood and sadness.

Robert's mother really only became aware of how Robert was feeling when she noticed that he was staying at home a lot, spending time alone in his room, and being more and more irritable with her and his sister.

Figure 2: Robert's vicious cycle

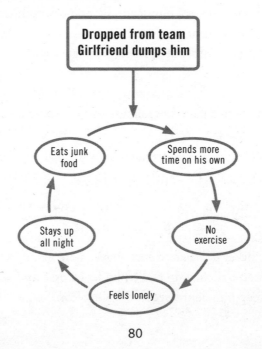

The initial 'trigger' for Emily feeling sad and unhappy was when she was bullied by girls at school. Emily's initial sad mood was noticed by the school nurse, who sent her home from school. Following this, Emily developed a lot of physical symptoms (tummy ache mainly) that made her worry about her health and meant that she stayed at home a lot. Her physical symptoms seemed to develop after Emily began to feel so unhappy. Because she was not at school every day she had more time to worry about them and this made her feel even worse. Emily's mother noticed that she was missing a lot of school and seemed really sad but did not know what had started this off until she asked more questions to find out what was behind the changes in Emily's behaviour.

Figure 3: Emily's vicious cycle

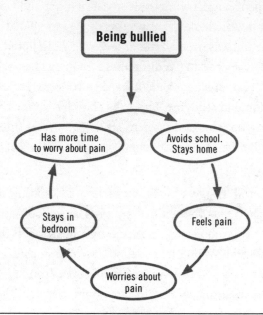

Lin moved to a new school and found it hard to fit in. She missed her best friend and felt very lonely. Lin tried to sleep to avoid her unhappy thoughts and feelings.

She spent hours trying to sleep every night and worried about how little sleep she was getting. She avoided being active and was tired all the time. For Lin, disrupted sleep made it increasingly difficult to manage her school-work. Lack of sleep made it hard to concentrate on her revision and studying. She tried to make up for this by staying up later and later to study. However, this only made her feel even more exhausted and she began to fall further and further behind. Her school marks began to suffer and this upset her and her parents, and became another source of her feeling bad.

Figure 4: Lin's vicious cycle

Everyone who experiences depression and low mood is likely to have a rather different set of experiences. However, there are often similar features and you might recognize some parts that are relevant to your own child. Some experiences are very common for teenagers and are often triggers for feeling low – bullying and other negative experiences with friends or other young people comes very close to the top. Similarly, most young people have pressure on them from schoolwork, and for many young people exams or competitions associated with hobbies or sports. These pressures can be managed well by most people when they feel well. However, they are a significant extra problem for young people who feel sad, unable to cope, useless or hopeless. As a parent you might not know about the specific trigger (if there was one) but you are likely to notice changes in your child's behaviour at home.

Below is a spare vicious cycle showing the key elements. You might be able to see how this works for your son or daughter.

Although a vicious cycle can feel impossible to escape from, in fact it usually does have exit points and these can show possible places to change. As this is a 'cycle' there's no right or wrong place to start to change. A change in any part of the cycle is likely to have an effect on the rest of the cycle so it can help to start wherever feels easiest. The focus in this chapter is to help you help your child to reset any of these key behaviours that have become problematic.

You may be able to sit down with your child and talk through some of the ideas in this chapter. This would be great. If you can we'd suggest that this is a good place to start. Ideally they

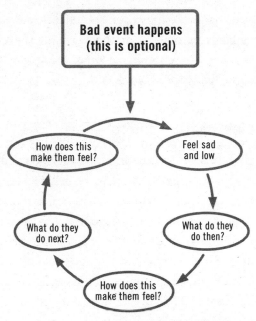

will agree that their sleep, eating or level of (in)activity is making them feel even worse. It might be useful to try to identify the vicious cycle that is keeping them stuck and then try to spot different ways to escape from it.

Once they make any change, however small, it is important to encourage and praise them. Young people who are depressed are very self-critical. They will tend to find fault with themselves, be very easily discouraged, think they are useless, be very pessimistic about change, and give up easily. With your support and encouragement they are much more likely to keep trying, to see any small change as positive and to simply stick with it.

It is quite likely, however, that your child will not be ready or able or willing to sit down with you and have a conversation about this. If that is the case then this chapter might give you ideas about how to provide some 'background' support to your son or daughter. There might be small things you can do to help your child get back on track with the basics.

Developing 'healthy habits'

When your child was a toddler and starting school it might have been relatively easy to get them into certain habits. You probably had family rules about bedtimes, mealtimes, and pastimes and activities. You may even have had a rule not to have strict rules about these things. In most families many of the structures and habits used to raise children came down to you from your own parents. Each family and each culture will have somewhat different ideas about what these habits should be, but to some extent these habits are also universal. We all need to sleep and to eat. There are general amounts of sleep that we need to manage well. Equally we all need a similar number of calories, and similar amounts of proteins and vitamins and fat to be healthy. Our bodies respond in very similar ways to physical activity and to exercise.

Many babies and young children find it hard to get into good habits of eating and sleeping. This can place considerable strain on parents and is something that many of us get help with. There are a lot of places to turn if you want help with a young child. These include people we see face to face, for example, our GP, health visitor, other parents and friends, and our own parents. It also includes people and support groups on the Internet – increasingly parents use each other to provide support and advice in this way.

All parents have to adapt to the changing needs of their children. Your role has to change as your child develops and it is usually difficult to get this right. However, although you need to behave differently as a parent of a teenager, many of the things you did when your child was younger are still broadly useful. Extending healthy habits into adolescence, and then into adulthood provides a solid basis for wellbeing and physical and mental health.

Looking after yourself too

Practical support and information is taken for granted when you have a young child. No one seems to expect you to get it right all on your own. It is not at all the same when you are the parent of a teenager. Now it can be very hard to know where to turn for help. As the parent of a teenager who is unhappy it may be even harder to know where to find help and support for yourself. If you are looking after an unhappy, sad teenager this has a big impact on you too. Do try to make sure that you look after yourself as well as your child.

Make sure that you are getting enough sleep, eating well, getting exercise and having a social life and support from other people. Not only will this help you get through a difficult time but it also provides a good 'model' to your teenager. 'Modelling' is a key idea in psychology. Children and adults learn in a number of different ways, including through rewards and punishments. They also learn many new behaviours and skills by watching other people. People who your child admires are likely to be more powerful models than people they do not admire. As you may already know, modelling works very well for behaviours you might not want your son or daughter to learn: for example, smoking, using bad language, and drinking alcohol. It also works for behaviours you do want them to learn and that you and other people demonstrate every day, including being kind to other people, practical skills such as cooking or DIY, taking exercise and keeping fit, and enjoying a social life. You are an important source of learning for your teenager – they are learning to be an adult and you are likely to be the most important adult that they know.

If you have, or have had, problems with low mood you will be able to empathize with your child. You may have learned coping strategies that might also help them. Importantly, you can show them how important it is to talk to other people, to ask for help, and to look after yourself.

You are what you eat!

Food is more than just fuel. It provides an opportunity to sit down and spend time together with family and friends. What we eat reflects the society we belong to; food plays an important part of religious and other social ceremonies and is a key part of many celebrations. What and how we eat can form a link between us and our culture and family background.

Most parents know that food plays a crucial role in developing a healthy body and maintaining good health throughout life. Most parents encourage their children to eat fruit and vegetables, to eat a balanced diet and to stay away from junk food most of the time. We all start off with the best intentions. However, life usually leads to compromises. Over time most parents become more relaxed about what their child eats. Sometimes, the diet of the whole family becomes rather unbalanced – working parents cannot always provide fresh home-cooked food. Many parents find it hard to afford fresh fruit and vegetables and simply do not have enough time to cook family meals from scratch every day.

The typical western diet has changed dramatically in the past few decades. Many more foods are available. Our supermarkets and street markets display a fantastic array of high-quality fruit and vegetables. However, many of our meals are now ready-made or processed. We now eat 34 per cent fewer vegetables than we did sixty years ago. Around 13 per cent of men and 15 per cent of women eat the recommended minimum of five portions of fruit and vegetables per day. People in the UK eat 59 per cent less fish than they did sixty years ago – decreasing the average consumption of essential omega-3 fatty acids.

This book does not aim to provide detailed advice on nutrition and health. However, if your child is experiencing low mood it may be useful to review how and what they eat and what opportunities you have to adjust their diet in ways that are manageable for you and for them. There are a number of reasons why this might be helpful:

- Helping your child to eat well may be something practical you can do to help them.
- The whole family will benefit from a well-balanced diet
- Mealtimes may provide an opportunity to spend time with your teenage children
- Cooking your teenager their favourite food is a simple way to show that you care for them

- Cooking and planning food can be a shared activity – many teenagers enjoy cooking or baking
- Some foods may have a positive effect on mood

Food and mood

Being depressed can really mess up your child's appetite. Poor appetite or eating too much are key symptoms of depression. Many people who are depressed report that they eat more, especially unhealthy, 'junk' food. Foods that are high in sugar, fats and starch give a short-term 'hit' or reward. Because they make us feel better, even if only briefly, food can quickly become a means of finding some comfort. But the quick-sugar rush with these foods can also lead to a 'crash' and an urge to eat even more of them.

Sometimes eating can just feel like too much effort. Eating may involve socializing and this can feel overwhelming. Others find that they lose their appetite completely and that when they are feeling depressed they lose weight.

Robert stopped eating his meals with the rest of the family and started eating alone in his room, especially late at night. Instead of eating the meals his mum cooked for the rest of the family Robert started eating a lot of pizza and other junk food. Not surprisingly, especially because he wasn't taking much exercise (he'd stopped playing football), Robert noticed that he put on a lot of weight.

Lin didn't feel able to eat school lunch with other people at school and started missing lunch. She lost weight and not eating during the day made her feel really tired.

Emily also avoided lunchtimes because she wanted to avoid the bullies. Because she didn't want to worry her parents she didn't say anything to them and when she felt ill she also didn't feel like eating.

A number of studies in the UK and Australia have studied the diets and mood of young people. For example, one project examined the diets of over seven thousand Australian children aged ten to fourteen years. After accounting for differences in family income, activity levels, age, gender and many other factors that might also be related, the researchers found a strong association between the quality of the diet young people ate and their mood. Young people with the least-healthy diet reported the highest symptoms of depression and those with the best diets reported the fewest symptoms of depression. A similar study published in 2013 found that in a group of three thousand adolescents from London, children with the least healthy diets were more than twice as likely to have symptoms of depression.

Studies such as these show a clear association between diet and mood but do not demonstrate conclusively that poor diet *causes* low mood – it could be that happier young people seek out a healthy diet or that unhappy young people seek out unhealthy comfort food. To test if a poor diet causes depression we would need to do an experimental study. This would be difficult and probably unethical as we would need to allocate some children to receive an unhealthy diet and some to have a healthy diet and then see what happened to them over the next few months and years. However, even if diet does not cause low mood a poor diet will certainly lead to other physical health problems. There seem to be plenty of reasons to help your son or daughter eat a well-balanced healthy diet – if there is also a positive effect on their mood then that's a bonus.

Research in nutrition and health has started to identify some types of food that seem to have a positive psychological effect.

Foods that contain flavonoids:

Flavonoids are found in a very wide range of fruits and vegetables. They influence the colour of the food and have a protective effect on many aspects of health including heart disease and cancers. Recently there has been much interest in the effects of flavonoids on mental health and mental functions including mood, attention and memory. Fortunately flavonoids are very high in many delicious fruit and berries including blueberries, strawberries and raspberries. Including other brightly coloured fruit and vegetables every day will ensure that your son or daughter has a wide range of different flavonoids.

Complex carbohydrates:

Carbohydrates make up a very large part of our daily diet and regardless of culture form the core of every meal. Because we eat so much carbohydrate, every day, what we choose to eat can have a major effect on our health. They are essential to health because as they pass through the digestive system, they are broken down into glucose – our brain's and body's primary fuel. Two categories are used when referring to carbohydrates, simple and complex.

Simple carbohydrates such as enriched flour, found in refined breads, pastas, and sugary foods, provide calories but few nutrients. They fill us up and can be associated with comfort and satisfaction. They are often found in junk foods and heavily processed foods.

Complex carbohydrate sources such as wholegrain breads, starchy vegetables and beans deliver fibre, as well as vitamins and minerals. As well as being packed with other good things, complex carbohydrates are digested more slowly and help us keep our blood sugar levels steady between meals.

How to rebuild healthy eating habits

If your child's diet has suffered while they have felt depressed this can contribute to the vicious cycle keeping them low. Whenever possible it is helpful to rebuild good eating habits.

You no longer have control over what your child eats and what they eat when they are not at home may not be something you can influence. Talking about food can be sensitive for some teenagers and some may see any attempt to take control of what they eat as an intrusion. You probably have a good idea of how your son or daughter is likely to respond to talking about how they eat and what they eat – use your judgment to decide how to approach this with them.

In any case, if you are still doing the main food shopping and your son or daughter lives with you, you can influence what they eat when they are at home. You, after all, are in charge of the food supply. If there isn't easy access to quick, less healthy food, your son or daughter will eat less of it. If there are alternative quick and easy healthy foods your son or daughter is likely to eat more of these. So this might be a good time to do a quick check of your food cupboards – are they full of crisps, biscuits, cakes, instant meals, pizzas, pies and chips? Over time, why not aim to replace the simple carbohydrates in your food cupboard with complex alternatives?

If your child had a physical illness and had lost their appetite you might try to tempt them to eat by preparing small amounts of nourishing, tasty, healthy food. You might also offer them small treats, foods that you know they like and would try to eat. Your own habits and behaviours are also very important. If you want to help your child to eat well you are the model they are most likely to imitate.

Here are some suggestions that may help you improve your child's diet and approach to food:

- If you are able to, eat together regularly. Mealtimes are important social events
- Encourage your child to eat breakfast – many teenagers get out of the habit of breakfast but experimental studies show that having breakfast improves mood throughout the day
- Be a good role model – what you eat and how you eat teaches your child a lot about food and nutrition
- Try and offer a range of different foods – be brave and experiment with foods you have not tried before
- Offer water with every meal and encourage your child to drink water between meals (and instead of soft drinks)
- If your child has no appetite offer them very small portions. This is less overwhelming and easier to manage. They can always have seconds

- It's better to eat little and often – several small meals may be easier for them to manage
- Do not keep junk food in the house. If it's not there it can't be eaten. Just making it hard to eat junk will reduce what you all eat
- Get rid of biscuits, cakes, sweets – have these on special occasions
- Many children enjoy baking
- Encourage your child to help you plan meals for them and for the family
- Plan a picnic for you and your son or daughter
- Consider learning to cook food from a different culture or country – your son or daughter might help you choose. This could be linked with a holiday, a film, or a lesson at school
- Teach your child to cook – if they can cook, encourage them to get involved in preparing meals. Cooking gives them more control and more knowledge
- Try using Internet resources to teach them to cook – they may find this more appealing than cookery books
- If you do get them a book try one for students – these are generally easy and focus on using cheaper foods
- Start with quick easy and healthy snacks and light meals. Simple cheap meals like beans on toast, daal and rice, and boiled eggs and 'soldiers' are fantastic and very healthy
- Tempt your child with food they might associate with happy times or when they were younger – 'eggy bread', for example, might appeal when other, more demanding or grown-up food does not
- Make your food look good and taste good

- Introduce new tastes and foods and try to extend the range of foods that everyone in the family eats
- If new food isn't popular at first be patient; it can take up to five different attempts before they start to enjoy a new food. So don't give up the first time, have a few more goes
- If your son or daughter is interested in keeping a record of what they eat, a food photo diary is quick and easy and helps keep a record of how your diet changes

Tackling problems with sleep

It's very common for young people (and adults) to have trouble sleeping. Many people who are not depressed also have trouble sleeping. It is normal to find it hard to sleep around important events, even positive ones like family parties or holidays. Excitement and anxiety can both keep us awake. One or two nights of poor sleep is fine – most young people can cope with that and catch up at the weekend. However, if your son or daughter has been sleeping badly for over two weeks this may be a good time to try to change things. In one study, young people who said they had sleep problems were four times more likely to develop depression so sleep can be an early warning sign as well as a symptom of depression.

The fact that sleep problems are so common makes it a useful place to start to change – telling other people that you have trouble sleeping can feel a lot easier than telling people you are depressed and unhappy.

How much sleep is enough?

About eight to ten hours a night is probably about right for most teenagers. Nine hours is a good average to aim for. This is a bit more sleep than most adults need and a bit more sleep than most teenagers get, most nights.

The amount of sleep we want and need is influenced by an internal biological 'clock' known as a 'circadian rhythm'. This internal clock is generally on a roughly 24-hour cycle and tends to be synchronized with the pattern of day and night. The circadian clock affects the time of day at which we feel tired, and ready to sleep, and how long we sleep, and when we would naturally wake up. There is some individual variation so that some of us prefer to stay awake later and sleep longer in the morning (so-called 'owls') and others prefer an early night and an early start in the morning (so-called 'larks'). Shift workers, people who travel to very different time zones, and those of us who stay up late at night socializing are all likely to experience the effects of disrupting this natural rhythm. Even changing the clocks by one hour in spring and autumn can take some time to adjust to.

During adolescence the circadian rhythm changes quite dramatically. Most teenagers have a distinct shift in the time at which they feel sleepy. They do not feel tired until around 11 p.m. and their natural rhythm is to go to sleep late and wake up later in the morning. Most teenagers are owls rather than larks. However, this does not fit with the usual school timetable. As a result, during school and working weeks most teenagers do not get enough sleep.

As a parent you are very likely involved in helping your teenager get up on time. They will rarely feel ready to wake at 7 a.m. and the lack of sleep that results means that as many as 25 per cent of teenagers fall asleep in class. Many teenagers 'catch up' with sleep at weekends and during the holidays. This is an opportunity for them to follow the rhythm of sleep that comes naturally to them.

Sleep and depression

The effects of sleep deprivation are known to anyone who has cared for a young baby. Lack of sleep makes us feel tired, more easily annoyed and irritable, and makes it hard to concentrate and to learn and to remember. Road traffic accidents, poor immunity to illnesses, weight gain, and diabetes are all linked to poor sleep. Sleep deprivation is also closely linked to low mood and depression.

Poor sleep can start before low mood and depression develops. In teenagers, poor sleep predicts the onset of depression. The reasons for this are not clear. However we can imagine that normal teenager experiences including pressure from exams and staying up late studying, or worry about a family member or friend, could trigger initial problems with sleep. Ironically, *trying* to get to sleep tends not to be very useful – the harder we try, the more sleep eludes us and the more frustrated and worried we become.

Poor sleep is also a symptom of depression and may occur only after low mood has developed. People who are depressed may find it hard to get off to sleep, perhaps because they have worries and thoughts going through their minds that keep them awake. Once they are asleep they may wake during the night, worry, find it hard to get back to sleep, and therefore not feel rested in the morning. In addition depression is associated with waking very early (too early) in the morning and not being able to get back to sleep. The cumulative effects of this disrupted sleep are obvious. Once sleep is a problem it is quite easy to see how it might become something that makes depression worse or keeps it going. Thoughts about sleep and the lack of it become another feature of depression – and another thing to worry about.

Young people who are depressed can develop disrupted sleep for different reasons. Robert, who found himself spending much more time at home alone, found that he was staying up very late, well after the rest of his family. Like many other teenagers he did not feel tired when the rest of the family went to bed. He played on his computer games right into the night, until 4 a.m. or even 5 a.m. When he finally got off to sleep he then didn't wake up till after midday. Not surprisingly he didn't feel ready for bed at 10 p.m. the next evening. After a couple of days Robert's internal clock got reset to a different rhythm from the rest of his family.

Other young people use sleep as a way of avoiding their sad feelings. Lin is a good example of this type of coping with low mood. Even when they get 'enough' sleep, young people who are depressed may find that they are not waking refreshed and feel tired all the time. They then try to solve their tiredness by doing less and less. This increases their depression and gives them more time to reflect and think about their problems.

How to help your child reset their internal clock

Tackling sleep problems can feel impossible. The trouble with finding it hard to sleep is that trying even harder to sleep just doesn't work. Lying in bed trying to get to sleep makes us feel more worried and anxious and less relaxed, this in turn makes it even harder to get to sleep. Getting into good sleep habits involves changing tack – trying harder isn't going to work – it's important to understand the basic way that sleep works.

If your teenage child is struggling with sleep difficulties they may be pleased and relieved to talk to you about this. However, it is also possible that they may feel criticized and told off. After all, when they were younger your role as their parent was to 'send' them to bed. Now your role is to support them to develop habits that work for them. To help them sleep better it is important that they are able to start to reset their internal clock. They will have to take the main responsibility for this and they will need your help along the way.

How to reset the internal clock

Your son or daughter first needs to decide what their sleep routine should look like. The average teenager will benefit from about nine hours' sleep a night. Therefore, if they have to be up at 7 a.m. to get to school on time they probably need to be asleep by about 10 p.m. All families have somewhat different schedules so it would be helpful for you and your son or daughter to discuss exactly what might work in your family. Whatever they decide to do they will almost certainly need your help and support.

During the first week, before trying to change anything, it can be very helpful to keep a sleep diary. This is good for a number of reasons:

- To find out exactly where things are now – i.e. how bad is it really?
- To highlight any areas where things are better (or less bad)
- To help focus on the sleep problem and take it seriously
- To compare with any change that happens so that you can see improvements
- To share information with other members of the family about the sleep problem

We have included a simple outline for a sleep diary that might be useful. There are also many other sleep diaries available on the Internet that you or your child might like to download.

My sleep diary

Complete the diary every day. It's probably best to do it first thing in the morning

Helping your child get 'back to basics'

	Day 1	Day 2	Day 3	Day 4	Day 5	Day 6	Day 7
What time did you go to bed?							
How long did it take you to go to sleep?							
How many times did you wake up in the night?							
After falling asleep how long were you awake for during the night?							
At what time did you wake up (the last time)?							
What time did you get up and out of bed?							
How long in total did you spend in bed?							
How well did you sleep? (1 = very bad, 5 = very good)							

Once you and your child have decided what a good sleep pattern would look like – for them – and you have a record of how they are sleeping now, it is time to agree on the target. So, for example, this might be that they need to be asleep by about 10 p.m. and awake by about 7 a.m.

The next step is to help them gradually alter their behaviour and habits so that they can start to move their schedule closer to the target. It is generally better to do this in small steps. So, for example, if your child is currently going to sleep extremely late, for example at 3 a.m. instead of 10 p.m., it would make sense to gradually move the time they go to sleep by an hour every few days. It might take several weeks to move them back to a 10 p.m. bedtime.

It is hard to get off to sleep if you are not tired. Therefore it is very important to help your child feel tired at the time they are scheduled to sleep. One important way to do this is to make sure that they start getting up earlier first. If your child agrees that their sleep is disrupted and agrees to try to tackle it they will almost certainly need help to start waking up earlier. This is where you come in.

By agreement (this is essential) you can help them in the hardest early days of resetting their internal clock. After a few days of waking earlier it will be easier for them to get to sleep a little earlier and their internal clock will begin to shift. During the day they may feel even more tired and irritable – this should be short-lived – but after a few days their internal clock will begin to reset itself and they will be able to get more sleep at night.

Sleep hygiene and habits

As well as resetting the internal clock it is also important to establish a good routine and habits around sleeping and bedtime. One key idea is to make sure that your child's bedroom is associated with sleeping, not with being awake and active. This might mean some changes to how things are arranged at home. Below are some key changes that you and your family might need to make to help your son or daughter start getting a good night's rest.

1. Tell your child not to worry about not sleeping well. She or he must accept that at the moment their sleep is disrupted but you both have lots of ideas about how to improve it.

2. Help your child cut down on caffeine. Teenagers often drink very large amounts of caffeine, mainly through soft drinks, but also in chocolate, coffee and tea. Teenagers who have had too little sleep may also use caffeine to help them feel alert the next day but this then makes it very, very hard to sleep well the next night.

3. Encourage your child not to drink any caffeine at all in the afternoon.

4. Beds are for sleeping in. Make sure that your son or daughter has a desk or table to do homework at and encourage them to use that. If it is in another room that's even better.

5. Encourage your child to watch downloaded films, check their social networks and so on somewhere other than on their bed.

6. Discuss with your child when and how they use their laptop, mobile, PC or TV. Negotiate a period of time before bedtime (e.g. thirty minutes) when they do not use these. Ideally put all screens in a different room before bedtime. Use an alarm clock, not a mobile phone alarm.

7. Make sure your son's or daughter's bedroom is comfortable and cosy. If you can, consider investing in new bed linen.

8. Keep to a regular routine around bedtimes. Encourage your child to get up and go to bed at the same time.

9. Set up a relaxing bedtime routine. Try to make this a quiet time so that your son or daughter can start to wind down. Baths, warm drinks, reading, lower lights, comfortable pyjamas, and quiet music can all help set a bedtime atmosphere in the lead-up to bedtime.

10. At bedtime remove all distractions. Shut the curtains; turn off music or other media. If your child shares a bedroom it might be helpful to work out how to stagger bedtimes or establish the same routine for their brother or sister. Your son or daughter might find it useful to use an eye mask so they are not woken up by the daylight early in the morning.

11. Set an alarm. In the morning help your son or daughter to get up as soon as the alarm goes off. They will feel tired. They are likely to be resistant and irritable. They will probably need your (gentle) help with this – be patient!

12. If your son or daughter does not go off to sleep and is

tossing and turning it is better for them to get up, out of bed and go into another room. They should distract themself with a quiet activity, e.g. reading a book, and then go back to bed and see if sleep will come. If it does not, after fifteen minutes they should get up again, read for a while and then go back to bed.

13. In the morning, draw back the curtains and let as much natural light in as you can. Daylight stimulates melanin, and this helps reset the internal clock.

14. Encourage your son or daughter to spend time in daylight during the day. Again, this will help reset their internal clock.

15. During the day, encourage your child to take exercise, walk, and be active. This will help them feel tired and sleep better.

Help your child eat regularly and at times that fit the **new** sleep/wake cycle.

It is often difficult to adapt to an earlier bedtime even if this is introduced gradually. If, after a few days, your son or daughter still finds it very difficult to get to sleep at the earlier time they should try going to bed an hour later but continue to wake at the earlier time. This is temporary. Your child has to need to be ready for sleep when they go to bed and it may take a while for their internal clock to shift. Put the alarm clock over the other side of the room. Help them to get up when the alarm goes off and get on with the day.

Other things to consider:

- Try cutting out all caffeine, alcohol or cigarettes
- Don't allow your child any naps during the day – keep all sleep at night-time and in bed!
- Increase your child's activity and exercise during the day
- Consider going to see your GP with your child – just talking about sleep problems to someone else might help you both see things a bit differently

Weekends can be a challenge for young people who are trying to improve their sleep patterns. It is important for them to understand that they need to be a bit stricter with themselves for a few weeks.

In particular **at weekends they should not stay up for longer than one hour after their weekday bedtime**. At weekends, in the morning, they should not stay in bed for **longer than thirty minutes** after their weekday waking time.

This is tough. But for a few weeks it is important because it will help get them into a good routine and reset their internal clock. Once they have had two weeks of good sleep they can start to be a bit more flexible. If they start having trouble sleeping they now know how to get back on track.

The more your child's sleep pattern is disrupted the harder it will be to change it and the more they are likely to need your help.

Robert's sleep pattern was really quite disrupted – he had shifted his bedtime by about five hours. He asked his mum to help him change but this was hard for them both because he got so irritable and snappy. They decided that they would gradually move his bedtime by an hour each day. Every day Robert set his alarm to go off an hour earlier. Some days he didn't manage to get out of bed when the alarm went off. His mum had to be quite persistent to get him out of bed.

Lin's sleep cycle was really confused. She went to bed as early as she could but then tossed and turned all night.

She was in bed for eleven hours every day and even longer at the weekend. Lin decided to start going to bed later at first. She planned activities to do until 11 p.m. at night for a week. Then she set her alarm for 6.30 a.m. and asked her mum to come and get her out of bed. As soon as she got up she dressed and took the dog out for a walk. The dog was very happy! Lin's mum helped her by making her breakfast while she was out.

You and your son or daughter need to work out what pattern will work best for them and for the rest of the family. If you are able to agree on the target, what steps to take and how you can help them this is most likely to work.

Exercise and physical activity

The benefits of exercise and physical activity throughout life are very well established and extensive.

Exercise – the pros

- Helps build and maintain healthy bones, muscles and joints
- Helps control weight, build lean muscle, and reduce fat
- Improves your skin
- Can help prevent or reduce high blood pressure
- Reduces stress
- Improves your mood

- Makes you think better and clearer
- Can help develop skills
- Can be done alone or with other people
- Boosts the immune system so you get fewer colds

Hidden in that list perhaps, but hugely important for your child, is the fact that exercise improves mood. After exercise you get a positive mood boost. This is a temporary boost, but the other benefits of exercise last longer – feeling stronger, fitter and leaner are all good for mood and for mental health as well as your physical health. Exercise, on its own, without therapy or medication, has been found to improve symptoms of depression. For example, eleven thousand people born in Britain in 1958 were followed up from the age of twenty-three to fifty. At all ages, those who took exercise reported less depression than those who did not take regular exercise. People who changed from inactive to taking exercise three times a week had a 20 per cent lower chance of developing depression in future. Those who became depressed were likely to have reduced the amount of exercise they took.

The importance of exercise for mental health and wellbeing is now widely recognized. The advantages are obvious – it is cheap, you can do it without a prescription, no professional help is necessary, it is flexible, it does not have long-term side effects, and can be adapted to fit into your daily life. Here's an example from the NHS website:

http://www.nhs.uk/Conditions/stress-anxiety-depression/
Pages/exercise-for-depression.aspx

For all these reasons we strongly encourage young people and their families to increase the amount of exercise they get. However, we know that although it is simple it is not easy. Taking exercise involves planning and motivation. When you are depressed it is hard to gather the energy needed just to open the front door and step outside. Simple barriers can seem impossible to solve and many young people feel hopeless and useless. So it is likely that they will need your help to become more active.

Your family will already have well-established patterns around exercise and activity. Children and young people learn behaviours and attitudes about exercise that are largely based on what they see their parents and family members do.

Let's check your family's approach to exercise.

a) We love exercise, it's something we all do and enjoy.

If you, the rest of the family, and your son or daughter who is depressed are still active that's great . . . keep it up. You already know that taking exercise makes you feel good. Having a regular exercise habit will keep you all fit, help you sleep, improve your appetite and your mood.

If your child is taking exercise three to four times a week as well as being active in everyday ways – walking, cycling, taking stairs rather than lifts, then they are doing great. It is particularly impressive if they have managed to keep this going when they are depressed. They must have some great skills to keep themself motivated and organized. If your child is exercising a bit less than this perhaps you could encourage them to step it up a bit? If they are taking gentle exercise, e.g. walking the dog, could they go a bit further or walk a bit faster? Is this something that could become more sociable or that you could help them with?

b) My son or daughter used to enjoy exercise but they've stopped and it feels too hard for them to get started again.

If your son or daughter has stopped taking exercise, there might be lots of reasons. Robert used to play football but stopped when he didn't get picked for the team. This was one of the things that seemed to trigger his depression. For Robert, exercise was not just a way of keeping fit but also a social event. He played with lots of friends and he loved being in the team and working hard together.

If your son or daughter has been low in mood and energy for a few weeks or months the idea of taking exercise again is probably horrifying. But they can almost certainly remember the up side of exercise and they may miss it but not be sure how to start again. If you can help them get back into the habit of taking exercise or being more active this will improve their mood and it will get easier.

One well-established way of treating depression involves increasing activities that are meaningful and important. We talk about this more in Chapter 7. If your son or daughter has enjoyed exercise before then this would be a good way to start increasing exercise gradually. If other members of the family are also active this will help encourage and support your child.

c) My child stopped taking exercise a few years ago. They don't seem to enjoy it at all.

Lots of young people stop taking regular exercise at high school. Girls are more likely to stop being active than boys. There are lots of reasons why young people don't want to do exercise, especially at school. These include feeling embarrassed, especially having to change in front of other people, having to wear school sports kit, getting hot and sweaty, and feeling clumsy or not being 'sporty'. If this sounds like your child it's likely that organized sport would be a big challenge. But they might remember other physical activities that they did enjoy – dancing, skate-boarding, playing with friends. This is a good feeling to get back.

If your son or daughter is not in the habit of taking exercise they might need some easy steps to try out. Problem solving can help identify some of the barriers and ways to overcome them. You and your child might find the chapter on problem solving useful.

We predict that if your child can identify the main barriers to exercise, with your help they will be able to find solutions and start trying out new forms of exercise that are closer to what they enjoyed as a younger child. Even if they hate the actual exercise, the physical effect of exercise can help their mood and help them sleep. This mood boost doesn't last but it does make it easier to try again and to keep going. Taking any exercise at all is a big step forward and a great achievement. It's important to recognize that and to praise any efforts they make.

d) They hate exercise – they've always avoided it. They're just not that kind of person.

If this sounds like your child there might be two options. First, they really do hate all sport and all exercise and are never going to enjoy it. If that's the case then it's important to make sure that they move around enough to keep their body working and able to last for the rest of their life. For them, physical exercise is just like car maintenance – important but not something to do more often than necessary. But it's important to find ways to move more in their normal life. Everyday moderate activity will help them to feel better, sleep better and build stronger bones and muscle. Walking to school, or to the shops, cycling rather than going in the car or bus, carrying shopping home, walking the dog, doing voluntary work, or helping with household chores all help to keep your child moving and active. Other hobbies and interests, including drama, might also involve more physical activity than they currently get.

Fitting activity into every day can be done as part of the activity log that we discuss in Chapter 7. The aim will be to fit activity around normal life so that it just becomes easy and automatic. Also the thought-checking section in Chapter 8, and the fact-finding section in Chapter 9, might be useful to help you test out some of the beliefs your child (and you?) have about exercise.

Second, it's also possible that your child just hasn't enjoyed exercise – yet. School sports tend to focus on competitive sports and team games. Your child might enjoy individual sports, such as running or gymnastics, or non-competitive sports such as aerobics, or other physical activities such as dance or yoga. They might prefer activities and sport with adults and older teenagers. This might be something you can also do or that they might start with another family member. It might also be easier to try out new things outside school, for example, yoga at a local sports centre or a club. Increasingly community activities including the popular parkrun UK are open to all ages.

Finding ways to help an inactive young person become more active is a challenge. This might involve being creative and trying out things you've not considered before. Brainstorming can help with thinking up new ideas and is a technique we'll talk about more in Chapter 9.

So, here's a summary – which type of exercise avoider is your child? How can this book help them become more physically active?

Exercise type	Next steps
A – It's one of the few things they still enjoy	Give them a pat on the back! What can you do to help them keep it up? Be generous with your praise and encouragement Offer practical support (e.g. lifts) to help them keep doing exercise

B – They used to enjoy exercise but it's hard to get going	Introduce exercise into everyday life – activity scheduling (Chapter 7) Praise all efforts, especially if they are not successful Consider your own habits – are you a good role model?
C – They've not taken exercise for years	Introduce exercise into everyday life – activity scheduling (Chapter 7) Identify the barriers and ways round them – problem solving (Chapter 9) Consider involving other family members – is this something the whole family might benefit from?
D – They hate exercise	Introduce exercise into everyday life – activity scheduling (Chapter 7) Are there other things that your child does or would like to do that would help them increase activity? Challenge negative beliefs about exercise – thought challenging (Chapter 8) Get creative, identify new ways of being active, problem solving (Chapter 9)

Starting small

The idea of 'taking exercise' can sound quite overwhelming when you are feeling low. This is especially true if your child has a long-term illness or disability that gets in the way of exercise. It can be particularly difficult if the rest of the family is not keen on exercise. But don't immediately write off the idea of your child becoming more active. Taking exercise can often help with the symptoms of a physical illness such as ME. It is never too late to start taking more exercise and this can be a good way for family members to spend time together.

What is really important is that your child is as active as **they** are able to be. You may need specialist advice to help you support them to take small steps to be more active. You may also need support from other family members, from school or from a sports club to give you the help you need.

Your child's activity is not just about moving their body around. It's also important for them to use their mind and to use this to discover new things and new possibilities.

Last word

This chapter aims to help you encourage your son or daughter to get back into some of the healthy habits you gave them as a child. Healthy habits that they can take into their adult life will protect them for many years. However, any change is hard. It is likely to take time to change their sleep, or their eating or their activity levels. Don't worry if this does not happen soon.

In general terms what is also helpful is for you to find ways to encourage and support them. Actions speak louder than words. Your behaviour and actions are likely to have more effect than what you say. Showing your care, love and concern is important. Words can easily be misunderstood, especially by a child who is depressed. Showing your love through behaviour, consistency and your presence remains important even during the most difficult times.

Your son or daughter may not always welcome your involvement – they may become irritable and angry, or see this as an extra unwelcome demand that you are making on them. You may need to restrict your involvement to making their environment at home somewhere that will support healthy rather than unhealthy habits. If they are not ready right now they might be next month or in six months.

Finally, look after your own needs and health. You are less able to support your son or daughter if you are not sleeping, eating or being active. Your example shows the way and if you have to change yourself, you also show it is possible for your child.

Part 3

Helping your child to get started

5

Why has my child become depressed?

Parent reflections:

'**It is not your fault that your child is ill**, but believe me you will at some point believe it to be. Parents with a strong sense of responsibility will beat themselves up that they should have noticed something earlier, got help sooner, done something different when they were young and so on. But you couldn't! And what would you have done if you'd known anyway? See? It was going to happen anyway. Ditch the guilt. It wastes valuable energy.'

When you have a child who is in distress or having difficulties it is natural and probably inevitable that you ask 'Why?' Or, more specifically, 'Why has this happened to my child?' The causes of depression are not always obvious and this chapter is written to try to help answer that question and draws on current research findings.

As a parent you can't help but wonder why your child is so unhappy. You may already have some idea about that or you may be completely mystified. Sometimes if we understand the causes of a problem we can find a way to solve them. This isn't always true, of course. Often the background causes are way back in time and we can't identify them. Or they are back in time but there isn't much we can do to change them. If you are more interested in finding ways to help your child just skip this chapter – you can always come back to it later.

Why has my child become depressed?

Depression often starts during adolescence. Adolescents are more likely than people of most other ages to become depressed. Until recently our understanding of this was pretty poor. Teenage depression often went unnoticed and most teenagers were not offered effective treatment. We still have a long way to go but we do now have a better understanding of depression in teenagers and why it is so common at this age.

All teenagers are living through a period of enormous physical, emotional, social and cognitive change. All of these changes influence their mental health and can be associated with depression. In this chapter we will describe how development and change in the teenage years is linked with depression and why young people are so vulnerable to depression at this time in their lives. As adults we can all look back at our own teenage years. Many of us remember, often with embarrassment, sometimes with regret, and occasionally with relief (that it's all over) those turbulent, self-conscious, exciting and scary years. As a parent of a teenager using those memories of our own experience can help us hold onto empathy for our child, who is now facing similar but possibly even more complex challenges.

Like many other physical and mental health problems depression has a number of different causes. These fall into three main factors: biological, psychological and social or environmental. In this chapter we will describe how each of these factors is related to depression in young people and you can see how well this fits with your own child.

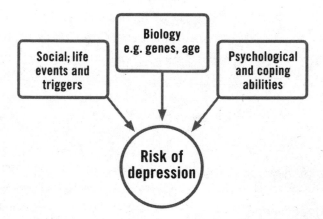

Most people who develop 'depression' have a combination of these causes. Each cause increases the risk that someone will develop depression but there is no single cause that guarantees that depression will develop. Depression can affect anyone at any age but there may be some additional factors that put teenagers at somewhat higher risk of depression.

Social factors: bad things happen, even to good people

Depression affects people of all races, cultures and classes. Depression has even been called the 'common cold' of mental health problems to reflect just how common it is. So anyone can become depressed, at any age.

Trigger events and life events

Trigger events

Specific events that seem to cause or 'trigger' a period of low mood or depression, and occur just before a period of low mood begins, are called trigger events. Typical events that can trigger depression include the following:

- Moving house
- Changing schools

- Parents arguing/family conflict
- Divorce of parents
- Being bullied
- End of a romantic relationship
- Feeling isolated.
- Feeling 'different', left out, shunned
- Someone loved moving away
- Serious illness
- Failing an exam or not doing well
- Someone loved dying or being seriously ill

On the whole, teenage triggers tend to be either to do with relationships with other people – friends, family, boyfriends or girlfriends – or about things to do with failure. Failure or fear of failing can occur in a range of areas, including school work, competitive sports and hobbies such as music or drama.

Some trigger events are brief and time limited. They can seem pretty minor and are often events that your child would usually be able to deal with. However, if your child is already feeling 'fragile' it may take only one more to tip them over into depression. In addition, triggers may be more important if the young person has also had a series of life events that have been challenging.

Life events

Life events change the course of our life in some way. They may mark a significant change or development. Life events can be positive and negative, planned or unplanned, and brief or long-lasting. Here is a list of the kind of life events that can be experienced by teenagers and may influence their wellbeing and mental health:

- Family member being ill
- Witnessing or being the subject of domestic violence
- Parent dying
- Death of brother or sister
- Discovery that one is adopted
- Starting a new job
- Birth of brother or sister
- Marriage of parent to step-parent
- Brother or sister leaving home
- Being excluded from school
- Parent becoming unemployed
- Becoming involved in drugs or alcohol
- Applying to university or college

The impact of life events adds up. Some people have a series of life events that they could have managed if they came along one at a time but which are unmanageable if they arrive in a close sequence. Life events can tend to pile up at particular times of change. So, for example, the birth of a baby can lead to other changes including stopping paid work or moving house. A new job for one family member can mean that the whole family must relocate, move schools, leave friends behind and deal with many new challenges. Life events can affect everyone in the family and include deaths, separations, family conflict including domestic violence, money worries and debt.

Some groups of children and young people experience many

negative life events and are at increased risk of depression and other mental health problems. These children include those who grow up in families who struggle financially or are relatively deprived, children who have experienced severe trauma, child refugees and asylum seekers, and children who are members of any social group that is not accepted in the wider community. Life events can also affect a whole neighbourhood or even a whole country. Wars, famine, natural disasters and poverty can all affect thousands or even millions of people and have a lasting impact on their mental health.

Some life events are of particular importance but their effects can be delayed. For example, women whose mothers died during their childhood are at particular risk of developing depression after they have their own children, especially if they have few friends and family members who support them. Many other events can cause young children to be separated from their parents. Illnesses, war, natural disaster and extreme poverty and deprivation can all precipitate separation. Although parental care and love is essential to the development of all young children, even this devastating event can be overcome. Young children are programmed to seek out care and to form 'attachments' to their carers. Even after traumatic separation children can develop new bonds with carers and develop a secure and caring relationship. It is important to recognize that even if your son or daughter experienced a difficult early childhood, they have the capacity to recover from this.

Psychologists who have studied life events have found that (as you would expect) people who report that they had a lot of life events happen during childhood are more likely to develop problems later in life. The world that children grow up in is rarely of their own making. They are influenced by decisions and events made by other people. Only as they get older do their own decisions become more important.

Robert, Lin and Emily all had different life events and triggers. For Robert, it was a combination of a trigger event, being dropped from the football team, and then the feeling of being left out, lonely, and breaking up with his girlfriend. For Lin, it started when she went to a new school. She missed her best friend and found it hard to fit in with the other girls. Emily's dog died and she was bullied at school.

You may be able to identify obvious triggers that your child has experienced in the last few months. They may appear to have caused your child to become depressed, or they may appear to have been 'the final straw'. Often a trigger event follows a sequence of negative life events.

So, children and young people who have experienced multiple, difficult and distressing events are at higher risk of developing depression. However, this is not a perfect relationship and many children who experience extreme events do not ever become depressed. The negative impact of major life events can be reduced if children feel supported by their family and friends, if they experience things improving, and if they are able to learn that they can cope and are able to manage, even when things go wrong.

The biological causes of depression – DNA, genetics and the brain

DNA and genetics

You might be aware that depression tends to run in families. Families share a lot of things, including their environment, and life events, and their genes. Depression, like diabetes, heart disease and many other physical and mental health problems, has a significant genetic influence. Therefore, if one family member is diagnosed with depression the chances are that they have a close relative who has, or has had, depression.

However, it has not been possible to identify a simple gene or combination of genes that puts people at risk of developing depression. Teasing apart the causes of depression is complicated. Not many diseases, if any, are 100 per cent genetically inherited. Identical twins are clones; they share 100 per cent of their DNA. Therefore, if a disease was 100 per cent inherited identical twins would always have (or not have) that specific disease. This does not happen with depression so depression is definitely not 100 per cent inherited.

The other reason why depression and other illnesses run in families is because families share a lot more than biology. Think about your own family. Consider the following questions:

a. Where do you live?

b. How much money do you have?

c. What do you eat?

d. What kind of school did you go to?

e. How much exercise do you get?

f. How many friends do you have?

g. How religious are you?

h. What type of job do you do?

The chances are you and the other members of your family have quite similar lives. You are likely to have a more similar life to your close family (i.e. parents, brothers, sisters) than to your wider families (i.e. your cousins, aunts and uncles). But all of you in the same family are probably more similar than you are to other random people. Most families share a lot more than genes. They live very similar lives. Because our diet, wealth, education, jobs, physical activity and social support all influence our physical and mental health, we are bound to share similar risks of depression.

In your family is there an illness that lots of your relations have had? A very common illness that is partly inherited is heart disease. Doctors will always ask about your family history of heart disease so that they know if you are at higher risk than average. Heart disease tends to develop when people are adults but lots of other health problems, like asthma, can start at a much younger age. Emotional problems, like anxiety and depression, are also known to run in families. If you are or have been depressed, or if your child is depressed, it is quite likely that other members of your own family have also had depression (even if they tend not to talk about it much).

The teenage brain

The brain develops and changes through our lives. However, there are two major periods of development and change. One period is during infancy. The brain of a baby changes very quickly and fundamentally and all parents have seen the effects of this rapid brain development as their child learns to control their body, sit, stand, walk and run, learn to communicate and learn a language (or more than one), begins to interact with people and animals, and to observe, understand and explore the world.

The infant brain also begins to learn how to process information and to respond to it. Young children exhibit strong emotions. Remember your child as a two-year-old? That is typically (and not just stereotypically) a time when young children express anger and frustration via regular tantrums. A key task for parents and children is to learn how to manage anger and frustration, ideally before the child starts school. Thankfully most of us eventually learn this quite well, which is why we often see a two-year-old having a tantrum in the supermarket but it is really quite rare to see a teenager or adult failing to manage their emotions quite so dramatically.

The second major period of brain development is between the ages of twelve and twenty-five. We see enormous physical change in our children as they reach puberty. At the same time there are equivalent changes in brain development that we cannot see directly. What you might notice happening, though, are changes in your sons' and daughters' advanced thinking skills. As they develop teenagers become much better at planning, thinking about the future, making judgments, thinking about their own behaviour and that of other people and managing the many demands placed on them as they mature.

Recent advances in psychology and neuroscience mean that we can now see how the adolescent brain changes and develops. We can use new methods of observing the brain, including MRI scanners. These can show us not only the shape and size of the brain and how this changes over time, but also the different areas of the brain and what areas are most active during different types of experience. This helps us understand better how adolescent development affects the behaviour, emotions and thoughts of teenagers.

There are key differences between the brains of teenagers and adults. Three areas may be of specific importance when we think about adolescent depression.

1. During adolescence the frontal area of the brain develops. The frontal region is where 'higher' order thinking skills are mostly based. These higher order thinking skills are critical to helping us manage our emotions and understand the world.

2. Neuroscience has also demonstrated that teenagers are highly sensitive to some external events and situations. They tune in to social cues and situations and are highly reactive in situations with their peers and friends. Most parents will have witnessed their child respond with

extreme emotion to even relatively minor disagreements with their friends. Similarly, feeling excluded by peers, or being bullied or ridiculed appears to have a highly distressing impact on teenagers.

3. On average, teenagers are more responsive to rewards than adults. Rewarding situations, often those which are inherently risky, like smoking, drinking alcohol, or taking illegal drugs may be more appealing to teenagers than to adults.

If we consider the combined effect of having higher thinking skills that are still developing, being more sensitive to social rejection or acceptance, and being more responsive to rewards, it is possible to see why adolescents can be uniquely vulnerable to their environment.

Young people are surrounded by very confusing, complex and competing demands. Their emotional response is well developed. They are highly sensitive to social rejection and acceptance and the many versions of social media they use mean that social cues can be everywhere, not just when physically with their friends. Rewards and temptations surround them. Young people are more able to reflect on their feelings and are more likely to try to make sense of the world around them. Your son or daughter may have a set of good habits and skills to help them find a way through these environmental demands but, not surprisingly, their skills are often overwhelmed by the demands of their environment.

Psychological resources and coping

The final area that can contribute to depression or protect us from it involves the resources and coping methods that the young person develops. These will be partly determined by their life experiences and learning opportunities. Psychological resources and coping contribute to us becoming resilient. However, this is not well understood by psychologists and even under the same circumstances and with shared genes brothers and sisters can differ in how **resilient** they are.

In this section we will talk about some of the ways people seem to be resilient, or 'hardy'. This is important because some elements of resilience can be learned and can then help protect against future episodes of depression. Characteristics of resilient people seem to cluster in three main areas:

1.   They have good **social support**. Social support basically means that they have family or friends that they can turn to for help. It seems to be more important to have a few really good friends or family, rather than a lot of friends whom you don't know well. Social media like Facebook and Twitter can give the impression that your son or daughter is well networked but these friends clearly are usually purely 'virtual'.

     Having good social support in your life means that you can ask other people for practical help to get over difficulties, and that you can accept comfort and sympathy when times are tough. Both aspects of social support are important.

2. They have balance in their life. Resilient people are involved in a range of different activities and relationships. They are the kind of people who don't necessarily put 'all their eggs in one basket'. If one part of life is going badly wrong, someone who has balance in their life is more able to access the good bits to help protect them. We will consider ways of increasing activity and balance and linking this to your son or daughter's values in Chapter 7.

3. Resilient people are optimistic rather than pessimistic. That means that they tend to assume that life will get better rather than worse. They may not be right, of course (!), but being optimistic seems to be very useful in warding off depression. Optimism and pessimism are two ways of thinking about the world and we will be coming back to this later in the book. CBT helps people to consider the way that they see the world, to collect and then evaluate evidence for their beliefs and then to reappraise their beliefs. We will discuss this at more length in Chapter 8.

The main aim of this book is to help you support your son or daughter to learn skills and habits that will protect them against depression and make them resilient. Our methods are all based on research that has been tested out both by scientists and by clinicians.

Why my child? – putting it together

As we've discussed depression is not caused by one single

thing. We have discussed the key background factors and some or all of these may be relevant to your child. But not all of the reasons are necessarily relevant – as we've already said everyone is different. If you are keen to figure out why your son or daughter may have developed depression you might want to put together your own explanation.

In CBT, the explanation for current problems is usually put together by the therapist and their client working in collaboration with each other. This is called a 'formulation'. Some therapists focus on reasons that are current, that keep depression going, and that can be changed. Others include reasons that lie in the past that cannot be changed but can help explain why someone is vulnerable. This can highlight possible future triggers or events that might lead to depression. This information can be used to develop a plan to avoid relapse.

We can see how this works for Robert, Lin and Emily.

Robert first:

Life events	Parents separated
	Dad has new family
Triggers	Not picked for football team
	Arguments at home
	Broke up with girlfriend
	Lost mates
	Trouble at school
Biology	Drinking alcohol
	Teenager, more sensitive to social rejection than adult
How he deals with things	Spends time alone
	Avoids people
Things that protect or help	Has a close family
	Wants to get back to college
	Sporty

Lin:

Life events	Family has moved a lot
Triggers	Started new school
	Misses her best friend
	Hasn't made new friends
Biology	Mum and sister have been depressed – possible genetic vulnerability
	Teenager, more sensitive to social rejection
How she deals with things	Keeps to self at school
	Sleeps a lot
Things that protect or help	Good student, wants to do well at school
	Creative

Emily:

Life event	Dad died many years ago
Triggers	Dog died
	Being bullied at school
Biology	Gets tummy aches, may have pre-existing vulnerability
How she deals with things	Cries, worries
Things that protect or help	Has been able to talk to her mum
	Has some close friends

If you've been able to recognize some of the factors that may be related to your son or daughter becoming depressed you might be able to work out an explanation that fits. This could be a useful exercise to do with them. In therapy this explanation or formulation would always be done after discussion between the therapist and client.

It is really important to encourage your child (and yourself) to think about things that might help protect them or that they could use to help them become less depressed. This might include using social support when they feel low, talking to family or good friends when things feel difficult or overwhelming, and things about them as a person (for example, being friendly, kind, thoughtful, likes animals, etc.).

My child

Life event	
Triggers	
Biology	
How I deal with things	
Things that protect or help	

Having an explanation that makes sense for your son or daughter and for you can help you to help them change. The rest of this book focuses on practical ways to help your child improve their mood. We hope it will also help you to understand a bit more about how depression affects young people and how to avoid it in the future.

6

The CBT principles

This chapter will outline the main principles behind CBT (cognitive behaviour therapy), with examples of how it applies to the understanding and treatment of depression. The ideas are very simple but can be incredibly effective. You may already be applying CBT strategies in your everyday life without even realizing it! The chapter also includes a section on developing a clearer understanding of the triggers and factors that may be keeping your child's depression going. Having a greater understanding of what may be keeping the depression going can be very useful because it will highlight the most important areas for your child and family to work on.

CBT is a treatment that is based on the idea that the way we think (the cognitive part) is closely related to how we behave and how we feel. These three areas are in fact so closely related that any shift in one will cause a cascading shift in the other elements. Some therapists refer to this as the CBT triangle:

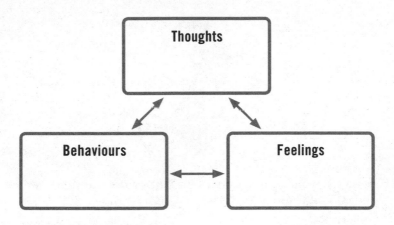

These interactions between our thoughts, feelings and behaviours happen all the time in every situation. Have you noticed how sometimes you and someone else might be in the exact same situation yet you both feel completely differently about it? We each think about things in specific ways and this then has an effect on how we feel and how we act. So it isn't the situations that we find ourselves in that determine how we feel, it is our **interpretation** of the situation that leads to our feelings about it and our responses.

Let us demonstrate with a simple example:

Emily's stepdad, Chris, knocks on Emily's door and pops his head in to say 'hi'. Emily looks up at Chris from her homework and shows a pained expression on her face without saying anything. She then goes back to reading her book. Chris pauses for a moment, not knowing what to do.

Chris's possible triangle:

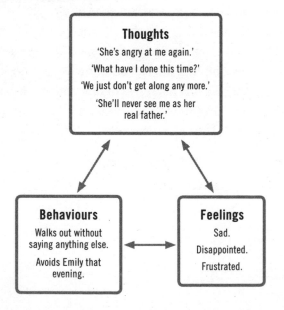

Chris's interpretation of the situation is such that it leads him to feel quite negatively and to act in particular (possibly unhelpful) ways. It's probable that you are thinking he has jumped to conclusions too quickly, or perhaps he could interpret the situation differently. This is certainly a possibility. He may be thinking in a particular way without having all the facts (more on fact-finding in chapter 9). So there could be other ways for Chris to think and interpret this situation:

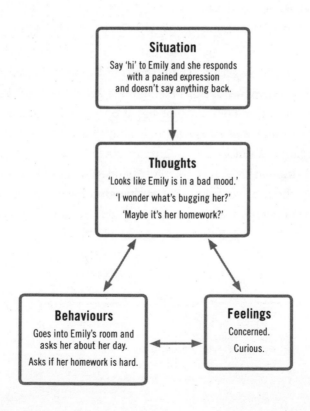

Situation
Say 'hi' to Emily and she responds with a pained expression and doesn't say anything back.

Thoughts
'Looks like Emily is in a bad mood.'
'I wonder what's bugging her?'
'Maybe it's her homework?'

Behaviours
Goes into Emily's room and asks her about her day.
Asks if her homework is hard.

Feelings
Concerned.
Curious.

It's possible that the second interpretation turns out to be right, or by talking with Emily, Chris might find out that she has a bad headache and that is why she has that expression on her face and doesn't want to talk. He may find out that she is angry for some reason and then he can talk to her about this further. The main thing to demonstrate here is that a simple shift in Chris's thoughts results in a change in his feelings and in how he responds to this situation.

CBT is all about firstly understanding and secondly changing a person's way of thinking and responding in order to change the way they feel (for the better). People who are depressed tend to see things in particular ways and their thoughts become quite negative. Their thinking becomes biased (e.g. jumping to conclusions or making huge generalizations based on something minor) and not based on the facts that are in front of them. They experience something that we refer to as Negative Automatic Thoughts or NATS. The thoughts are called automatic because they just happen without the person willing them to come up. These thoughts have a big impact on how a person feels and what they do. So you can see that someone with depression can get locked into unhelpful cycles pretty quickly:

Robert's mum noticed that Robert often got caught up in the following unhelpful cycle:

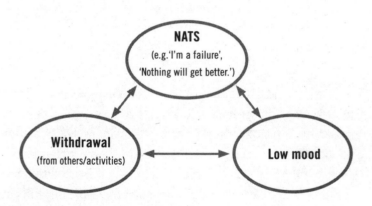

Another way of showing this cycle is by separating **physical feelings** and **emotional feelings**. You may recall from the introductory chapter that depression can cause a number of physical symptoms such as tiredness, sleeping problems or concentration difficulties. The following diagram is sometimes referred to as a HOT CROSS BUN:

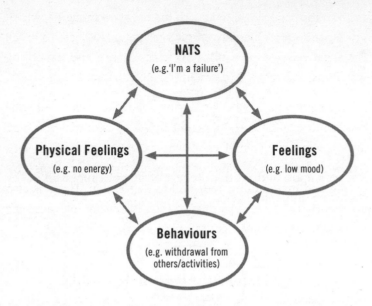

You may be able to see that in the example above it would be useful to take a closer look at Robert's NATS and ways of thinking and his ways of responding/his behaviours. NATS can be evaluated in terms of how realistic they are. Robert feels he is a failure but it's probable that there are many things that he has not failed at. Similarly, the absolute belief that **nothing** will get better is perhaps not based on facts and reality and there may be a more balanced way of looking at things (more on this in a later chapter about tackling unhelpful thoughts).

In terms of how Robert is responding, we can see that withdrawing from other people and activities may be understandable given his low mood, but it may also be keeping his low mood going. Not engaging in activities may reinforce Robert's belief that he is a failure and at the very least, it will give more opportunities for him to spend time alone with his negative thoughts, which gives rise to more negative thoughts. Helping Robert to break the negative cycle by re-engaging in activities is also something we discuss in a lot more detail in the next chapter.

At this point you may be wondering about the cycles that your own child may be getting caught up in. In addition, you may also be wondering about your own cycles (we all have them!). Below we help you to consider the things that are perhaps triggering and maintaining your child's depression. There is also an opportunity to see whether your child's cycles interact with your own, which may highlight further areas for change.

Developing an understanding of my child's depression

You may have already gained a better understanding of what has led to your child's depression in the previous chapter 'Why my child?'. Depression is complex and there may have been many different things that have contributed to the difficulties your son or daughter is experiencing. It is useful to understand these past contributing factors but it is even more useful to examine the factors that keep things going now. We can't change what has happened in the past, although we can develop a better understanding, but we can certainly make changes to what is happening 'in the here and now'.

Have a think about the following questions. If possible, you may wish to work through these questions with your child so that you both increase your understanding of the depression.

1. Are there any current triggers to your child's low mood that seem to make the depression worse?

(Examples: being on their own for too long, events at school, bullying, interactions with particular people, stressful situations, going on social media sites, family stresses, sleeping problems)

2. Does your child experience particular thinking styles that make the depression worse?

(Examples: always predicting the worst, seeing the negative side of things, making huge generalizations from small things, seeing things as hopeless, being overly critical about him or herself, expecting things to be perfect)

3. Does your child respond or cope in ways that seem to keep the depression going?

(Examples: avoiding people, avoiding activities previously enjoyed, putting things off all the time, using alcohol or drugs, setting overly high standards and expectations for him or herself, stopping exercise, spending long periods of time on gaming, avoiding making decisions)

4. Are there things that are preventing your child's depression from getting worse?

(Examples: still attending school, support from family, still sees a couple of friends sometimes, manages to do some enjoyable activities, motivated to get better, using strategies or getting help from professionals, has people to talk to, less stress)

5. What changes may help to reduce my child's depression?

(Examples: changing thinking styles and patterns, changing the way my child responds to their low mood, reducing withdrawal, engaging in exercise, stress reduction, finding more support, getting family more involved, tackling things that were previously avoided, family members making changes)

If you have found it difficult to answer the questions above that is perfectly fine and not unusual. It may take some time to find the answers and some of the chapters in the rest of this book may help you with this. You can come back to this section as many times as you like and add additional ideas as they come to you.

Opposite, we have included some blank cycles for you to fill in for your child's examples. If your child is willing, he or she may be able to help you to fill these out together.

My child's cycles

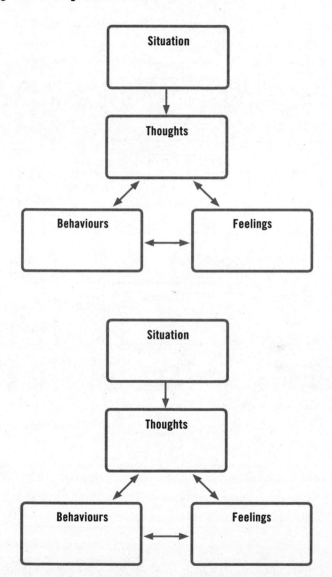

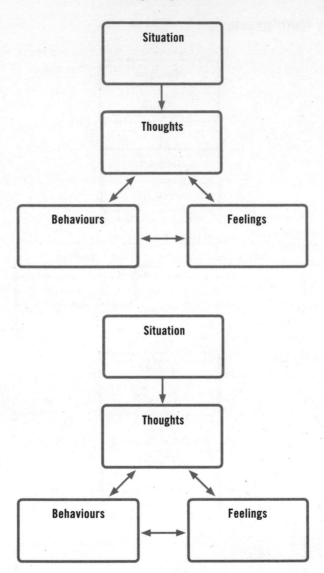

My own cycles

You might want to take the opportunity to have a think about your own cycles in specific situations with your child:

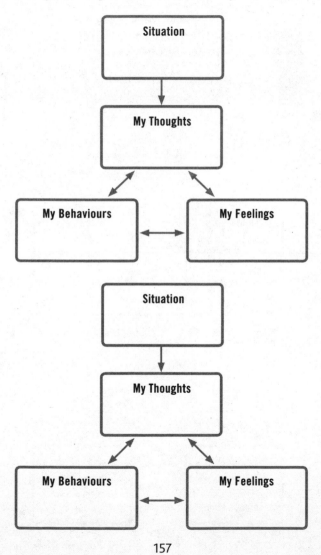

Now have a think about whether your child's and your own cycles ever get tangled up together, to form a bigger cycle?

For example:

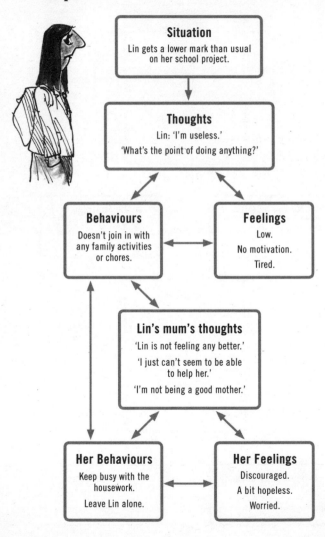

Situation
Lin gets a lower mark than usual on her school project.

Thoughts
Lin: 'I'm useless.'
'What's the point of doing anything?'

Behaviours
Doesn't join in with any family activities or chores.

Feelings
Low.
No motivation.
Tired.

Lin's mum's thoughts
'Lin is not feeling any better.'
'I just can't seem to be able to help her.'
'I'm not being a good mother.'

Her Behaviours
Keep busy with the housework.
Leave Lin alone.

Her Feelings
Discouraged.
A bit hopeless.
Worried.

The CBT principles

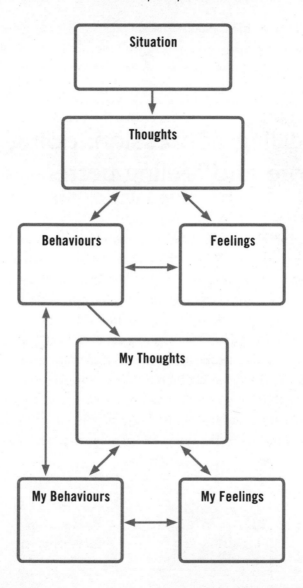

7

Tackling depression: doing more and feeling better

This chapter is all about helping your son or daughter become more active. We used to think that the lack of activity associated with depression was just a symptom of depression. Treatment focused on understanding the causes of depression, trying to change thoughts and feelings alone, or using medication to treat depression. It was assumed that if treatment was successful that the symptoms of depression, including low levels of activity, would then improve. However, recent clinical research has shown that lack of activity is not only a result of depression, but that it also keeps depression going. Lack of activity maintains the symptoms of depression and may make them worse.

Remember Robert? In Chapter 4 we described a number of specific trigger events that made him unhappy and miserable. He wasn't picked for the football team and his girlfriend dumped him and started going out with one of his friends. He was understandably sad and felt awkward with his friends. Normally Robert would have been busy at the weekends and evenings, he would have spent time with his friends, and their company would have distracted him and cheered him up. Playing football meant he was part of a team and the exercise and social activity involved were both good for his mood. This time Robert didn't feel able to spend time with his friends. He felt embarrassed and a bit humiliated. He didn't have the demands of being in the football team and as a result he spent a lot more time on his own, at home.

In Chapter 4 we discussed the benefits of physical activity and exercise and suggested that most people feel better if they are more active and busy. We also described the vicious cycle of depression, low activity and increased depression.

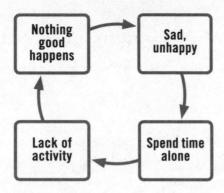

The knowledge we have about the benefits of activity and exercise and the negative effects of being inactive has been developed further and used as a specific treatment for depression in adults. In formal clinical trials this form of treatment – Behavioural Activation (BA) – has been shown to reduce the symptoms of depression and to be as effective as other psychological therapies. It is also much simpler and straightforward. There is not much formal research yet on the effects of behavioural activation for teenagers who are depressed. However, our recent clinical experience using BA has been very encouraging. Young people and their parents find it easy to understand BA and the effects on mood of using BA appear to be positive.

This chapter extends and builds on the basic relationship between inactivity and low mood. It will suggest different ways that your son or daughter might be able to try to help get out of their vicious cycle of inactivity. It will also focus on linking activity and behaviours to your son or daughter's interests, goals and values.

In this chapter we will focus on the following:

- Why doing more will help your son or daughter start to feel better
- How to start an activity log
- Helping your son or daughter to identify their personal values
- Supporting your son or daughter to increase activities that link with their values and goals
- Using other people to help support your son's or daughter's activities

If you want to just get on with things straight away, turn to the section about keeping an activity log and you can get going with that. If you want to find out more about why doing more will help your son or daughter feel better, read this part first.

Why doing more will help your child start to feel better

One of the things we know about depression is that it is hard to keep doing normal activities. Young people who are depressed do not just suffer from low mood. They lack motivation and energy. They feel hopeless and useless. They may be sleep deprived, and have a poor diet, both things that will make them feel even more tired and worn out. Depression interferes with work and school life, with getting on with friends and family members, and with enjoying their normal activities.

Robert used to be really active and very sociable. He loved playing football and spending time with his friends. As he started to feel low, he stopped lots of his normal activities and began to spend more and more time alone at home. And what about Lin? She used to enjoy spending time with her sister and mother, going shopping, drawing and seeing her friends. She spent a lot of time doing her school work and was really proud of getting good marks. Now that she is depressed she doesn't do any of these things any more. Opposite is a list (not exclusive) of activities that will be part of everyday life for many young people. Which of these did your son or daughter used to do? How many do they still do?

Activity list

Physical activity	Do now?	Used to do?
Swimming		
Playing sport (e.g. tennis, football)		
Dancing		
Other physical activity (e.g. riding, running, cycling)		
Skills/work/education	**Do now?**	**Used to do?**
Learning to drive		
Paid work (e.g. babysitting, paper round)		
School		
Homework		
Music lesson		
Creative things	**Do now?**	**Used to do?**
Drama		
Art (e.g. painting, drawing, sculpture)		
Playing music		
Cooking		
Writing (e.g. stories, diary, poetry)		

Being sociable/relationships	Do now?	Used to do?
Watching TV with family		
Having a family meal		
Shopping with friends		
Voluntary work		
Spending time with family and friends		
Having fun	**Do now?**	**Used to do?**
Going to the cinema		
Playing computer games		
Going to a party		
Having friends to stay overnight		
Planning a party or social event		

If life started getting better for your son or daughter now, what things do you think they would start to do again? Are there any activities that they might start doing for the first time?

People who are not depressed usually have a lot of different things they look forward to and enjoy. This means that if they stop doing one thing they always have other things to look forward to. However, people who are depressed tend to do far less. They spend more time alone, do fewer things that they enjoy, and have more time to think about their difficulties. Robert and Lin both stopped doing things that they enjoyed and started spending more time at home, mostly on their own. At home, alone, they have more time to think, more time to feel low, and much less to distract them from their low mood.

Why do we do less and less when we feel depressed?

Being depressed is hard. Everything is an effort, things aren't so enjoyable and we feel rubbish. It's easier just to stay at home than it is to go out. Even getting ready to go out can feel like too much effort. The things we used to enjoy don't excite us as much as they used to and our motivation and levels of energy are low. This makes it hard to force ourselves to do things that we might enjoy.

Then if we miss something once it's a little bit harder to go back the next time. If we miss the next time, that makes it even harder to go back, and even easier to stay at home. Unless someone or something gives us a little push we gradually start spending more time at home and do less and less.

Sometimes there are specific reasons why we stop doing things. Robert used to enjoy playing football and spending time with his friends. Then he got dropped from the football team and one of his friends started going out with his girlfriend. Suddenly it was hard to go back and play football or to spend time with his friends. He felt embarrassed about the team – he wondered if he'd exaggerated his football skills. Maybe his friends and the coach had never thought he was good at football. Was he a fraud?

Robert was also upset about his girlfriend going out with his friend. He didn't want to be reminded that she now had a new boyfriend and he definitely didn't want to see them together. He decided it was less upsetting to avoid the football team and to avoid his friends. And in the short term maybe it was easier, but after a while he found he was stuck, he missed his friends and he missed going out, but it was hard to change anything.

Avoidance and how it makes things worse

It's natural to avoid things that hurt us or are upsetting. We all do it and it can make a lot of sense. We avoid danger all of the time. As parents we teach our children to avoid danger. We show them how to cross the road safely, help them recognize situations that might be risky, give them the tools and the information they need to keep them safe. Sometimes we avoid things that we find upsetting or painful. This can be useful too.

But sometimes avoidance starts out OK but then starts adding to our problems. It can be like that in depression. Robert stopped seeing his friends and playing football because it was easier for him. To start with he did feel a bit better. He was relieved that he didn't have to face his friends and didn't have to worry about what they would think and what he would say to them. After a little while Robert missed all the good things about being with his friends and playing football. He didn't think he could talk to his friends about how he felt. He didn't know what to say to them about why he'd missed football practice. He was embarrassed about how he felt and didn't know how to handle this.

From a distance it's much easier to think about lots of other ways of dealing with Robert's difficulties. Of course he could have joined another football team, or gone and made new friends at college, got a new girlfriend, or started doing something completely different, like a part-time job. But these things can be hard to do, even when you feel happy and energetic. When you are depressed they can feel **impossible**!

So: Less energy + less motivation = less activity = depression

Why doing less makes us feel worse

It's not obvious why doing less increases low mood and keeps depression going. The short-term solution seems reasonable – we are avoiding being hurt and upset. After all, in other situations, when we are physically ill, we are told to go to bed and rest. So sometimes doing less can be good for us. Why isn't that the case when we are depressed?

There are a few reasons.

1. When we are less active and do less we have less chance to enjoy ourselves. We have less fun. As psychologists, we would say that we get less **positive reinforcement**. Positive reinforcement is anything that makes it more likely that we will repeat an action. So, for example, if every time I go for a run I feel good, then I am more likely to go for a run again. Positive reinforcement of an activity simply means that we are likely to do that activity again. When we are inactive we have far less opportunity to receive positive reinforcement – therefore we are likely to continue to be inactive.

2. When we are less active we are less likely to spend time with other people. Other people, especially our friends and family, are usually good at helping us enjoy things. They might join in on fun activities, give us confidence to try something difficult or new, praise us or recognize when we are working hard at something, or make us laugh.

3. If we spend more time alone and do less, we have more time to worry and think about our problems and less to distract us from thinking about them.

This kind of repetitive, circular thinking is called **rumination**. Rumination is a kind of stuck thinking – it tends to go around in circles and not come up with solutions to problems. Rumination tends to focus on things in the past and how they went wrong. It can include thinking like 'What if I hadn't . . .', or 'What if they had done . . .' Rumination is not problem solving – it is going round and round a problem without making any progress or solving anything.

Lack of positive reinforcement, lack of contact with other people and rumination combine to make us feel worse – this is the depression trap and it looks a bit like this:

The depression trap

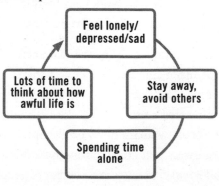

Why start with activity? Why not focus on thoughts and feelings?

Depression is a complicated disorder that typically includes a range of different symptoms and experiences. During times of depression, just as in the rest of life, our emotions, behaviours and thoughts are all connected. If we change one thing (for example, our thoughts or beliefs), this has an effect on all of the other things.

What's the reason to start with a focus on changing behaviour? Quite simply, we think it is easier to change behaviour than to change thoughts and feelings. As individuals we have more direct control over our behaviour than over our thoughts and feelings. As a parent, you can see what your teenage child is doing – you cannot see what they think or what they feel. You may be able to infer their thoughts or feelings and your child may tell you how they feel and think. But sometimes it's just not that easy. It can be very difficult to describe how we feel. Our emotions can be confusing, mixed and complicated. Our thoughts can be fleeting, jumbled, hard to pin down, frightening and private. Even if they could, your teenage child may not want to talk about their feelings and thoughts.

If your son or daughter did talk about and describe their feelings to you, would it make sense to start by trying to change their feelings? It seems logical to focus on bad, unhappy feelings. People often think that's the place to start. It's why they sometimes say that people who are depressed should 'snap out of it', or 'cheer up', or even, 'pull yourself together'. If only it was that easy! Frankly, if it was that easy, the number of people who were depressed would be very much lower. Your teenager would simply need to give themselves a good talking to and that would be it – they'd be better. You wouldn't be worried about them, you wouldn't be reading this book, and you wouldn't feel so baffled.

> Cheer up,
> it might never happen!

OK, if you were able to read your teenager's thoughts, or if they were able to capture them and describe them to you, would it make sense to try to change them? Perhaps – but capturing thoughts and then trying to alter them can be tricky. We prefer to start with simpler things. Later in this book we do consider in more detail how your child's thoughts may be contributing to their low mood and we look at different ways to challenge unhelpful thoughts. It's also relevant to think about your own thoughts, including your thoughts about your child and their low mood, about your responsibilities as a parent, and about your relationship with your son or daughter.

Helping your son or daughter do more (and then a little bit more)

When we as therapists are working with young people who are depressed we can be quite direct with them. We work hard to develop a good relationship with them, to find out about their experience, to empathize with them, and to listen to what they say. This helps us to identify their goals and things that they want to change. It also helps us encourage them to try things that are difficult and that they do not want to do, like becoming more active.

This is not easy to do. However, it is easier to do this as a therapist than it is as a parent. As a therapist we have the advantage of being a stranger, a professional and an adult. Many young people find it much easier to talk about their difficulties with someone outside the family.

So we do not assume that as a parent you will be able to use the direct approach. If you are able to sit down and work together with your son or daughter that is helpful. The next section is for you, but it is based on the material in our book for teenagers, *Am I Depressed and What Can I Do About It?*

1. Help your son or daughter understand the link between activity and low mood

It isn't easy for someone who is depressed to start being more active. Lack of energy, motivation and hopelessness can interfere with any plans or suggestions that you may make. So it is important that your son or daughter understands the relationship between low mood and lack of activity. Simply understanding why doing more might be helpful is an essential first step towards change.

Explaining the link between activity and low mood may be easy for you to explain and for them to understand. If it is not, you might find it useful to give them a few pages in this chapter to read. Alternatively, they might like to look at our book aimed at teenagers, mentioned on the previous page. Sometimes it's easier to accept new information if it comes from a neutral source, like a book.

2. Help your son or daughter to start an activity log

At the start of this chapter we offered a list of common activities. It is likely that your son or daughter is doing very much less than they once did, and probably less than other teenagers. The first step to increasing activities and improving their mood is to establish what they are doing now. For that reason we suggest keeping an activity log. Once your son or daughter has a record of their starting point, the aim is to help them to increase their activity level.

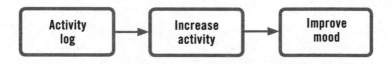

The activity log will help your son or daughter (and you) to

- Identify their activity starting point
- See links between their activities and their mood
- Spot times when they could start to be more active
- Show changes in their activity level (and mood) as they progress

So, what does an activity log look like? It really is nothing complicated. There's one over the page to give you an idea but it is also very easy to make your own. You can download these from the Internet, but the diary or calendar on a mobile phone might be easier and useful. If your son or daughter is willing to keep an activity log make sure you are really positive about this. They are taking a big leap forward and overcoming lethargy, low mood and pessimism so it's important to acknowledge this.

When your son or daughter is ready to start recording their activities be prepared to offer help but do not insist on it. It is important that they know you want to help, even if they refuse to accept it.

It is important for them to try to record all activities. This means anything and everything, including 'doing nothing'. In an activity log, there is no 'nothing'. Things like sleeping, thinking, sitting alone, waiting for a bus, watching TV, or trying to sort out problems all count.

Then they should try to rate how each activity made them feel, from 1 to 10:

a. How enjoyable it was – 1 is not at all and 10 is hugely enjoyable.

b. Their feeling of achievement – 1 is not at all and 10 is a massive achievement.

c. If it made them feel closer to anyone or anything else – 1 is not at all and 10 is if they felt much, much closer.

d. how important it was – 1 is not at all and 10 is very important.

We recommend keeping the activity log for a week, including weekdays and a weekend. Your son or daughter may want to share this with you or to keep it private. If they find it hard to remember what to record, discuss with them how best to remind them. Encourage them when they complete it. Don't worry too much about getting it right – getting started is much more important. They can always try again if they don't manage it first time.

My activity log – today's date _____

Date, time	Activity – what I did, with whom and where	Achievement	Closeness	Enjoyment	Important?
7 a.m.–8 a.m.					
8 a.m.–9 a.m.					
9 a.m.–10 a.m.					
10 a.m.–11 a.m.					
11 a.m.–12 noon					
12 noon–1 p.m.					
1 p.m.–2 p.m.					
2 p.m.–3 p.m.					
3 p.m.–4 p.m.					
4 p.m.–5 p.m.					
5 p.m.–6 p.m.					

Tackling depression: doing more and feeling better

6 p.m.–7 p.m.	7 p.m.–8 p.m.	8 p.m.–9 p.m.	9 p.m.–10 p.m.	10 p.m.–11 p.m.	11 p.m.–12 midnight	12 midnight–1 a.m.	1 a.m.–2 a.m.	2 a.m.–3 a.m.	3 a.m.–4 a.m.	4 a.m.–5 a.m.	5 a.m.–6 a.m.	6 a.m.–7 a.m.	7 a.m.–8 a.m.

Activity log: troubleshooting

- If activity monitoring for the whole day is too hard, encourage your son or daughter to do it during the day, little bits at a time

- It might be easier to do this on their phone

- Try setting reminders on the phone at intervals during the day

- You could send your child a text message to remind them

- If they can't see the point of it, encourage them to just let that thought go

- Consider the activity log as a bit of an experiment – it's something to try

- If it doesn't work, don't worry

- Could a brother, sister or friend help encourage your son or daughter?

- Would your son or daughter find it easier if someone else filled it in for them?

A completed activity log

So, what does a completed activity log look like? Over the next few pages you'll see a day from Lin's activity log. Naturally your son or daughter will have a different set of activities and experiences. You will also notice that it's not filled in exactly as we suggested earlier. Lin found it hard to rate everything – so rather than decide how important her activities were from 1 to 10 she decided to just say Yes (Y) if they were important and leave it blank if they were not important. Feel free to be flexible – your son or daughter needs to find a way that suits them.

Lin's activity log

Date, time Monday 8th	Activity – what I did, with whom, and where	Achievement	Closeness	Enjoyment	Important?
7 a.m.–8 a.m.	Overslept – woke up late, felt awful.	0	0	0	
8 a.m.–9 a.m.	Got dressed, ran for bus, missed breakfast.	0	0	0	
9 a.m.–10 a.m.	First lesson – maths x 2, forgot homework.	0	0	0	Y
10 a.m.–11 a.m.	Break. Sat in library on my own. English lesson.	2	0	1	Y
11 a.m.–12 noon	English lesson, History lesson. Sat next to Emma.	4	3	3	Y
12 noon–1 p.m.	Lunch – ate with Emma. Talked about her gran.	0	6	4	Y

1 p.m.–2 p.m.	Science practical. Worked with Claire and Sam.	5	3	5	Y
2 p.m.–3 p.m.	Science practical. Got homework.	5	3	3	Y
3 p.m.–4 p.m.	Home on bus. Sat on my own.	0	0	0	
4 p.m.–5 p.m.	In my room. Felt sad, cried. Didn't do homework.	0	0	0	
5 p.m.–6 p.m.	Went to dance class.	2	4	5	Y
6 p.m.–7 p.m.	Teatime with family. Brother got school prize.	0	5	4	
7 p.m.–8 p.m.	In my room, supposed to be doing homework, cried.	0	0	0	Y

Time	Activity				
8 p.m.–9 p.m.	Watched TV with brother. Dad came home.	0	7	7	
9 p.m.–10 p.m.	Packed school bag, set alarm, had a bath, got ready for next day.	4	0	3	Y
10 p.m.–11 p.m.	Went to bed, said goodnight to family.	2	2	2	Y
11 p.m.–12 midnight	Couldn't get to sleep.	0	0	0	
12 midnight–1 a.m.	Tried to sleep, got up, had a drink, went back to bed.	0	0	0	
1 a.m.–2 a.m.	At some point went to sleep, took ages.	0	0	0	
2 a.m.–3 a.m.	Asleep.				

Let's have a look at Lin's activities. This was a school day so she was quite busy and a lot of her activities were important and hard for her to avoid. Lin didn't enjoy much of the day but the most enjoyable part was in the evening when she was watching the TV with her brother. She spent a few hours in her room on her own, sometimes doing homework (or not doing homework).

Her day is probably not unusual. Your son or daughter might spend a lot of time most days doing things they have to – going to school, homework, exams, part-time jobs, hobbies and sports. All of these things are important but they can make it hard to find time to do things that are enjoyable or things that make them feel closer to other people. Routine activities can even squeeze out more enjoyable activities.

An ideal activity log would include a balance between doing important (and unavoidable) things, doing enjoyable things just for fun, and doing things that help build family relationships and social networks. Having a good balance of activities provides more support for young people, makes them more resilient, gives them more opportunities to develop important skills, and encourages them to develop independence.

Making sense of an activity log

After a few days, ideally a whole week, encourage your son or daughter to review their activity log. They may be willing to share it with you or may want to keep it private. Either way it's useful to ask the following questions:

- How many different things did you enjoy?
- How many of your activities were important?
- Do your activities give you a feeling of having achieved something?
- Do any of your activities make you feel closer to other people?
- Is your mood the same all the time, all through the day from morning to evening, or did it go up and down?
- Was your mood better or worse than you expected (or about the same)?
- Was your mood the same every day?
- Did your mood change at particular times?
- What were you doing when your mood was most positive?

Linking activities and values

Increasing their activity level is not likely to be helpful to your son or daughter unless these activities are meaningful to them and increase their exposure to positive reinforcement. Activities that are meaningful and reinforcing are typically linked with your child's values. As they develop from a child to an adult your adolescent child will develop and refine their values. It's very likely that many, perhaps most, of your child's values will have been shaped and influenced by you and your family. Some will be picked up in the wider community, from school, from friends, from watching TV and reading. Our values help define who we are, contribute to our identity, and inform our actions and decisions. Adolescence is a key time when our values and identity are forming so thinking about their values and discussing these with you can help your son or daughter develop that part of themselves.

To help adults and young people identify their values we highlight three areas that are often important.

- **You** (hobbies/fun, physical health, looking after yourself)

  We suggest that people who are depressed think about the values that relate to themselves first. This is because we want to emphasize that they, as an individual, are important and valuable. We want to avoid the tendency many depressed people have of putting themselves last, of denigrating themselves, and of being self-critical and self-hating. So first of all we encourage depressed young people to think about activities that may help them feel healthier and happier. This can include eating, sleeping, taking exercise, self-care and grooming (make-up, hair, clothes), watching favourite TV programmes, having a really good meal, reading a great book, or going for a walk. It doesn't need to be ambitious. At this stage, your son or daughter may find it easier to imagine doing things that will make them healthier – it is likely to be very hard to think of anything that would be enjoyable or fun.

- **The things that matter** (education/work, things I need to do, the 'bigger picture')

  Everyone has things that they need to do. This includes working and studying. Young people have a huge number of demands placed on them by school, parents, and sometimes employers. They may also have serious hobbies that require commitment and energy (e.g. music, sport). Additional tasks and demands include new life skills (e.g. learning to drive). Also, don't forget about the 'bigger picture'. This includes doing voluntary work, politics, religious activities and working to improve the environment.

- **The people who matter** (family, friends, boyfriend/girlfriend)

Spending time with family and friends and offering emotional support and practical help are important activities. Social interaction helps us and other people. It is particularly important to have support from other people when times are hard. This is something that reduced activity can also make more scarce and which can further increase low mood. It's also important to give other people support and help when they need it.

If your son or daughter can identify their values in each area and then find activities that match them they will start to develop a good balance. This balance across different areas will help increase the amount of positive reinforcement they receive, this will then make it more likely that they repeat the activities, improve their mood and confidence, and develop resilience.

Values can sound rather vague and woolly. Opposite is an example of Lin's life values. You and your son or daughter might find it useful to use this as a basis to start discussing what might be important to them.

Lin's life values

What is important to Lin about each of these areas?

Me	Things that matter	People who matter
Hobbies/fun	**Education and work**	**Family**
I'd like to continue dancing and get a bit better	Work hard, do well at college and get a good job	Make my family proud of me Be a good sister
Keeping healthy	**Things I need to do**	**Friends**
I want to be able to be strong and fit so that I can carry on dancing	I want to be more creative and find time to write Look after my family	Be good to other people Be kind and thoughtful
Looking after myself	**The bigger picture**	**Boyfriend/girlfriend**
Maybe I should make sure I do enough things for myself	Make a difference to other people – improve things	I'd like to have a boyfriend

On the next page is a blank sheet for you and your son or daughter to complete.

My life values

What is important to you about each of these areas?

Me	Things that matter	People who matter
Hobbies/fun	Education and work	Family
Keeping healthy	Things I need to do	Friends
Looking after myself	The bigger picture	Boyfriend/girlfriend

Starting to be more active

We know that changing behaviour and becoming more active is hard but we also know that if your child can change his or her behaviour and become more active it will help them to feel better and less depressed. So it's important. This is where he or she really starts to change.

It's particularly difficult to know where to begin. In the activity log you might see lots of times when your child could increase their activities. But how do they decide what to do and when? Have a look at your child's activity log and their life values. How well do they match?

Values tend to be quite general and abstract. Here are some of Lin's values:

'I want to make my parents proud.'
'I want to do well at college and get a good job.'
'I want to be a good sister.'
'I want to stay fit and strong so that I can carry on dancing.'
'I want to be more creative and have time to write.'

How well do Lin's values match her activity log? Can you see any areas where she could add activities or change her activities to match her values a bit better? We can rate the match between Lin's activities and her values out of 5.

0	1	2	3	4	5
No match					Perfect match

What three simple activities could Lin add that would help her match her values?

Lin's life value	Match	Possible new activity
Make my parents proud.	4	No
Do well at college and get a good job.	4	No
Keep healthy.	3	Yes – exercise more?
Be a good sister.	3	Yes – spend more time with brother?
Be more creative.	0	Yes – add one hour a week to write or draw.

Lin now has at least three new activities she could add that would be a good match for her values. There's no right or wrong place to start so it's a good idea to start with things that are easier and things that are more likely to be enjoyable. She can then gradually add activities over a few weeks. It might be easier to add activities at the weekend, when there is usually more free time, than on Monday to Friday. Or she could add some activities, like texting her sibling, on the bus journey to school.

Your son's or daughter's activities and values

Going back to your son's or daughter's activity log it may be possible to match up their activities to their values. Looking at their activity log for a week is there an activity that matches each of their values?

My life values

This is what I did (from the activity log) to match my values

Me	Things that matter	People who matter
Hobbies/fun	Education and work	Family
Keeping healthy	Things I need to do	Friends
Looking after myself	The bigger picture	Boyfriend/girlfriend

Your son or daughter might find it hard to recognize how their activities match their values. They may tend to underestimate the value of what they do. Don't worry too much if this is hard for them. Being depressed interferes with concentration and attention. It also makes us underestimate our abilities and efforts and to remember more negative things than positive things. Your support and encouragement may help identify matches between their activities and goals.

Where are the gaps between their activities and values? If your son or daughter has activities in most of their values they are doing very well. They may not recognize how well they have done already to try to overcome their low mood. You might want to comment on this and to congratulate them on doing so well.

It's more likely that your son or daughter has a few values where their activities are quite low. These might be opportunities to start to increase their activity. At this stage it is really important to take things very slowly. Your son or daughter will find it hard to do more than they already do and will be quickly discouraged. They may feel hopeless about the possibility of change. If you or they set ambitious targets that they cannot meet there is a danger that this simply discourages them even more.

Tackling depression: doing more and feeling better

Life value area	Rating 0, 1, 2 or 3	Possible new activity
1		
2		
3		
4		

Increasing activities – troubleshooting

If it is difficult for you and your son or daughter to decide where to start, here are some ideas:

- Start with something small and simple

- Activities that relate to self-care might be easy to organize and show an immediate effect, e.g. getting a haircut, having a manicure

- If they are not taking any exercise, gently increasing physical activity might be a good place to start. What about walking the dog or walking to the shops?

- Consider including other family members in the activity that they choose

- Activities that your son or daughter values may not be things that you yourself value – for example, they may enjoy spending time playing a computer game and you may not consider this an 'activity'. But it is. It should be included in the activity log just like any other activity

- Are there things in their activity log that they enjoyed more than other things? Can they do more of that?

- Have they stopped doing something that they did enjoy? Why not start again?

- Are there activities that would help match more than one of their values? For example, can they combine doing something for themselves, like keeping healthy, with spending time with people?

- What about things that are just for pleasure – this could include creative activities like playing music, art or drawing

- Check that they include activities that are relaxing

- Include activities in the evening that will help them wind down for bed

- Try to include some physical activity every day. If they can spend time outside, that's great

- Make a plan. Think about the next seven days and help them to add one extra activity each day. Ten extra minutes a day is plenty to start with

- Plan extra activities and write down the plan

- Start small. It's better to do an extra activity for ten minutes and get it done than to aim to do fifty minutes and give up halfway through

- Try to let other family members know what your son or daughter is trying to do. They can help in lots of ways – giving new ideas, encouragement, praise, general support, practical help, suggestions and joining in with activities

Keeping going

Getting started is a huge achievement. It's very important to reward your child and to encourage and support their progress. Try to focus on their efforts, rather than their results. Encouragement can be verbal or non-verbal. Paying attention to your child, smiling, nodding, and doing the activity with them can all help encourage and support them.

It's great to see you having a go at that.

Talk to your son or daughter about what they find encouraging and what you could do to help them try things out. Consider what practical obstacles might exist as well as any worries or fears that might be getting in the way.

Your son or daughter may tend to minimize or underplay their progress and focus on and exaggerate any failures. This is the effect of their low mood and can undermine their motivation to continue. Their activity log will show what they have achieved and is an important way to track progress. You and your son or daughter will see what activities are going well and what effect different activities have on their mood.

It can also be helpful to think about increasing their activity as an experiment. The aim is to find out what effect doing more activity has on your son's or daughter's mood. You will be collecting information about their mood and their activity to find out more about the relationship between their mood and their activity level. This is important. If you both consider that the aim of being more active is to make them feel better, you are in danger of setting an aim that is too ambitious and which you will feel you missed.

Your son or daughter is likely to feel that change is impossible for them. Part of being depressed involves negative thoughts about the world and the future. They will also be sensitive to failure and a setback can trigger further thoughts about hopelessness, how impossible it is to change, and how useless they are at everything. Try to pick small, easy, simple activities. A five-minute walk that is achieved successfully is much more helpful to your son or daughter than a more ambitious thirty-minute walk, which ends after twenty-five minutes.

It can also be helpful to encourage them to try things out, 'just to see what happens'. If you want to suggest an alternative approach or different activities using phrases that invite questioning and doubt and do not assume that there is a right answer or a right response, this will tend to open up possibilities rather than close them down.

I wonder if ...

Could it be that ...

Approaching doing more as an experiment means that if it doesn't work that the experience can be thought of as something to learn from rather than proof that your child cannot change. If your son or daughter is not able to complete the activity you planned with them, remind them (and yourself) that this is an experiment. What did they learn that could help plan the next activity? Perhaps you were a bit too ambitious? Or maybe the activity didn't seem to make sense? It may be useful to involve someone else to help your son or daughter or to have a treat at the end.

Here are some other things that might help keep things going forwards:

- Involve others. Activities that involve other people can be harder to avoid so, if you can, encourage your son or daughter to plan activities with others. A bit of gentle peer pressure (encouragement!) can help get them over small hurdles and barriers. Also, they might be able to find activities that help them get closer to other people and match their other values (e.g. keeping healthy).

- Congratulate your son or daughter when they manage an extra activity. This is really important and they are making real progress. Build in little treats or rewards for you both. You deserve it.

- Encourage them to continue to record their activity and mood; use the activity log each day. Make sure that you find time to sit down together to discuss what the information is showing you.

- Your interest and involvement is really important. By

spending time with your child, helping them and paying attention to their activity log, you are showing them in a real, direct way how much you care. What you do to show you love them and care for them is much more powerful than what you say to them about how much you love them.

- If you have a setback, reduce the level of activity a little so that it is manageable. Progress need not go in a straight line.
- Don't compare your child's activity level to what other people are doing
- Check that your son or daughter's activities are a good match to their values
- Try to make sure that they are able to separate their values from yours – there will be overlaps but they are also likely to be different
- Give yourselves a break. No plan works perfectly. Things will go wrong for all sorts of reasons.

8

Thoughts on trial: helping your child tackle unhelpful thoughts

Parent reflections:

'This is a huge step [having that first conversation about your child's depression], but the work is only just beginning. What you need to do next is to "be in it together". What I mean is, be willing to suffer along with your child. You do not leave them alone with it. It might sound weird to say you must be willing to suffer along with your child, but you are literally and figuratively setting out on a journey together. Together. You do it together. In the same way you remind your child to brush their teeth, you sometimes have to say, "Hey! You're doing that 'all or nothing' thinking thing again, remember?" Keep it light, keep it humorous but keep aware. Somewhere along the journey both you and your child will grow and change. That is why it is so important to be together. You will both benefit from being aware on this journey.'

As we described in Chapter 6, this book uses the key methods and ideas from Cognitive Behaviour Therapy (CBT) to help you help your teenage child with problems of low mood and depression. The relationship between our thoughts (cognitions), feelings and behaviour is close and powerful.

Imagine that thoughts, feelings and behaviours were all part of a mobile, connected to a single hanging point in the ceiling. Any movement of one part of the mobile is picked up by all the other parts; pulling one part disturbs all other parts. Thoughts, feelings and behaviours are connected in a similar way. CBT makes use of this connection to effect change in uncomfortable, unpleasant and distressing feelings, including low mood and depression, by changing behaviours and thoughts.

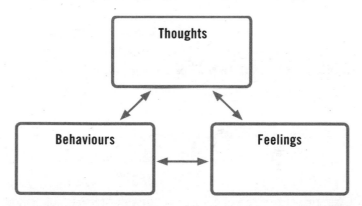

In this chapter we will focus on the C of CBT – **Cognitions** (or thoughts). Cognitions refer to a range of mental events. Unlike your son's or daughter's behaviour, which you can see, cognitions are private, internal events. You cannot directly observe anybody else's thoughts although you can sometimes infer or guess what they might be thinking because of what they say or do.

It is not always that easy to identify even our own thoughts. We are pretty much thinking all of the time we are awake but most of this mental activity happens automatically and without us being really aware of it. What goes on in our minds includes verbal thoughts that can be positive, neutral or negative. For example, 'I'm rubbish', 'What shall I have for dinner?' and 'I love that dress' are all verbal 'cognitions' or thoughts. Cognitions can also be word-free – often we have images or pictures that come into our minds. Smells, sounds, and sights can trigger strong images that are often linked to memory. Cognitions can be free-flowing, can be triggered by specific events or experiences, and can focus on the past, the present or the future, and be deliberate or automatic.

A really powerful thought might include a combination of pictures, smells and sounds. So, for example, try to bring to mind a time when you went to the park in the summer for a picnic. Perhaps close your eyes. Let the images come into your mind. Who else was there, what was the weather like, what food did you have to eat?

If you spend a bit of time on the memory a whole range of thoughts about it might come to mind – the smell of grass, the texture of the grass against your hand, the size, shape and colour of the trees, or the picnic rug, the faces of the people you were with, the sound of an ice-cream van or children playing in the background, the taste of the soggy sandwiches in your mouth. The more different ways we have of remembering things, the stronger and more real they can feel.

The power of thoughts lies in their variety and flexibility and in the fact that they determine how we interpret the world. In this chapter we will:

- Show how thoughts can lead to depression and keep depression going
- Identify common thinking traps
- Help you and your child catch the thoughts that are making them feel worse
- Challenge their thinking traps – are they reasonable?
- Develop and strengthen more helpful thoughts
- Learn how to ignore or let go of 'stuck' thoughts

How do thoughts lead to depression and keep depression going?

Negative thoughts have the power to change our behaviour and our feelings.

Depression has a lot of symptoms. One key symptom is negative thinking. People who are depressed typically have negative thoughts about themselves, about the world, and about the future. This is known as the 'cognitive triad'.

Imagine this situation.

It's Saturday morning. You hear the postman at the door. On the doormat is a yellow envelope addressed to you. You open it – it's an invitation from old friends you haven't seen for several years. They are having a party in six weeks. You are free that evening and they live close by so you wouldn't have any problem getting to the party.

> # You are invited to a PARTY

What does that make you think? There are many different thoughts that might come to mind – here are two examples:

Option A   Option B

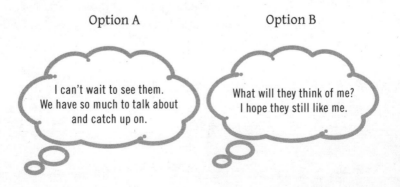

I can't wait to see them. We have so much to talk about and catch up on.

What will they think of me? I hope they still like me.

Straight away we can see that these two different thoughts could make us feel very differently. Thought A is likely to lead us to feeling excited and happy. Thought B makes us feel a little bit worried and a bit anxious.

In this situation the initial thought has a direct effect on our mood and feelings. Other thoughts could have a different effect on how we feel. Because our thoughts can be so varied and so creative, almost every situation can be thought about in a different way. And these different ways can lead to lots of different kinds of feelings.

Thoughts help us interpret and make sense of the world

Two important facts about the world around us mean that we all have to take shortcuts in our thinking.

Information overload!!! First, we are bombarded by information in the world around us. This has probably always been true and people have evolved to be able to filter out useless or irrelevant information. In the twenty-first century we have almost infinite access to information. Some information is vital if we are to stay alive. Most of it is really just noise. Therefore, through the process of evolution we have become skilful at ignoring a lot of information and attending to information that suggests danger. To do this we use a lot of shortcuts to help us ignore irrelevant information.

Caution! The world is full of unclear information! Second, a lot of information around us is unclear or ambiguous. When something is unclear we have to work harder to understand what it means. Some ambiguity is built directly into the English language.

Read these words out loud. As you do so , think about the meaning of the word and try to picture the word in your mind. Or put the word into a sentence so that it makes sense.

Sink / Bed / Bark / Mummy / Rock / Shoot

Each of these words has at least two different meanings; they look the same and they sound the same but they mean something different. Without more context you can't tell which meaning is intended. Some of them (e.g. sink, shoot) have one meaning which is more negative and one that is more positive. Did you pick up on the positive meaning or the negative meaning of those words?

Biased interpretation in depression

What's really interesting is that our mood can influence how we interpret ambiguous information. People who are depressed or worried are far more likely to interpret ambiguous situations or words as negative. So in the example above they are more likely to visualize a boat sinking rather than a place to do the washing up (sink) and a gun rather than part of a plant (shoot).

In contrast, people who are not depressed have a tendency to see things as less negative or more positive. So if they read those words out loud they would probably see a place to do the washing up (sink) and a plant or flower (shoot). Generally, people who are not depressed tend to have a view of the world that is more positive than it actually is. For example, when surveyed, about 75 per cent of people think that they are an above-average driver. Is this possible? Obviously not – lots of people must be wearing rose-tinted glasses when they imagine themselves driving.

Psychologists call this tendency to take something unclear and to lean towards seeing it as more negative or more positive as a **thinking bias**. It is completely normal to have a thinking bias – this is just a tendency to lean one way or another in our thinking – towards the positive, or the negative. It's as if some people are looking at the world through a pair of brown- or grey-tinted glasses and other people are looking at the world through a pair of rose-tinted glasses.

A very well-known kind of thinking bias is a glass half-filled with water.

Is the glass half-full? Or is the glass half-empty? Obviously it could be either – neither bias is 'right' or 'wrong', they are just taking a different perspective. The information could go one way or the other – it's ambiguous and we need to inter-pret what it means to make sense of it. People who have depression tend to make negative interpretation biases. This means that when information is unclear or could be nega-tive or positive in meaning that they will tend to interpret it as negative.

Here are some examples of ambiguous information. Your task is to read each one and decide what is going to happen.

a. You are going to see a good friend at the station. You
    haven't seen her for a long time. You feel emotional think-
    ing about how much she might have changed.

b. It's New Year's Eve. You think about the year ahead of
    you. You are in a thoughtful mood and think back to past
    achievements and disappointments that you have experi-
    enced during your life. What are your main feelings?

c. It is a cloudy day and you are sitting on the beach. You look
    up to notice the weather really beginning to change.

OK, great. You might be able to imagine a range of possible
outcomes. Some of them are positive, some neutral and some
negative. Opposite is a set of responses from a teenager with
depression.

a. You are going to see a good friend at the station. You haven't seen her for a long time. You feel emotional thinking about how much she might have changed.

    What if she has turned nasty?

b. It's New Year's Eve. You think about the year ahead of you. You are in a thoughtful mood and think back to past achievements and disappointments that you have experienced during your life. What are your main feelings?

    Scary, horrible memories and scared of the future.

c. It is a cloudy day and you are sitting on the beach. You look up to notice the weather really beginning to change.

    It's probably going to rain.

What you immediately notice is that these responses are all making a negative interpretation of the situation. The situation itself is ambiguous and it could be seen as negative, neutral or positive. When someone is depressed they are much more likely to see the negative meaning or interpretation.

Biased attention in depression

Other important biases that can have a direct effect on how we feel and behave are also seen in depression. We've already mentioned the importance of attention – we need to pay attention to things that are dangerous or harmful. If we don't we could get damaged or hurt before we even notice that there is danger around.

Consider where you are right now. If you stop and pay attention, you will notice many different things happening. You might be able to hear the radio, traffic, people talking, music playing, birds singing, the central heating pump, dogs barking, or all of these things at the same time. Normally you tune most of this background noise out and you do not pay it any attention. This tuning out happens quite automatically without you even noticing it. Our ability to automatically tune out irrelevant material is really quite remarkable.

If you are a driver you might have experienced this ability to change focus. Under normal conditions we can drive along safely, listen to the radio or to music, carry on a conversation and break up an argument in the back seat. However, when traffic conditions, or the weather deteriorates, and driving becomes more difficult or demanding we 'tune out' unnecessary information. Because we need to pay attention to the road, to be alert, and to monitor other drivers more carefully all of our attention becomes focused on this task. We automatically pay attention to things that are more important – in this case, our safety.

Imagine a teenager who is frightened of dogs going to the park to join their friends for a picnic. In the park what do they look out for? Probably dogs.

They are more vigilant and more attentive to dogs than their friends. They notice all the dogs in the park. They monitor where the dogs are, how far away, what size they are, if they are on leads, and if they are coming closer or moving away.

Paying attention to every dog in the park takes quite a bit of attention and effort. This leaves much less attention and effort for doing what they came to the park for – to have a laugh with their friends, have a picnic, and enjoy themselves. Because checking all the dogs all the time is quite an effort and not very enjoyable it's likely that they will decide to go home earlier than they need to. Going home and getting away from any dogs is much easier than staying in the park and constantly being on high alert.

So what we notice and what we pay attention to directly affects how we feel and often what we do. Also, when we pay attention to certain things we ignore a lot of other things.

Biased memory in depression

In research experiments people who are depressed, and even those who are just temporarily a bit fed up, are more likely to remember negative information and less likely to remember positive information. We can test this with standardized materials so that the effect of our personal history and experiences is removed.

Read the adjectives in the box overleaf:

Clever	Cheerful
Stupid	Pathetic
Skilful	Successful
Bright	Respected
Useless	Pitiful
Unwanted	Incapable
Trustworthy	Kind
Confident	Weak
Kind	Loser
Interesting	Lovable
Failure	Worthless
Amusing	Friendly
Feeble	Foolish

Now close the book for a moment and then write down as many of those words as you can remember (no cheating!).

How many did you remember? How many positive words and how many negative words? Did you remember more positive words or more negative words?

Depressed people, and those who have had an artificial mood 'induction' to make them feel sad for a brief period, tend to remember more negative adjectives than positive ones. In contrast, people who are not depressed or who have not been put into a sad mood tend to remember fewer negative adjectives and remember more positive ones.

What does this mean? It means that our memories are biased by the mood we are in – if we are in a sad mood most of the time, as we are if we are depressed, our memories will generally tend to be biased towards the less positive things that we've experienced. We will remember fewer of the good things that have happened, and more of the bad things. This is likely to make us feel worse. Naturally, the effect of our memory bias is that our sad mood continues for longer.

Thoughts are often 'automatic' and hard to notice

We are thinking virtually all of the time. But much of this thinking is in the background and we are not even aware of it. Like music playing in the background we can tune in and out of our background thoughts. When we do not tune in to it, our thinking plays on automatically.

This doesn't matter if our thoughts tend to be mainly positive or neutral. But as we've seen above, when our mood is low or we are depressed our automatic thoughts tend to be biased in a negative direction. This means that if your son or daughter has had a period of low mood and depression, they have been having negative, automatic, thoughts (NATS) in the background for much of the time. In addition their attention is likely to be focused on more negative things and their memories are likely to be biased towards unhappy or negative times in the past. The combined impact of this negative thinking is to increase low mood and depression.

Likewise, because our thoughts, feelings and behaviours are all connected (remember the hot cross bun?), these automatic negative thoughts also change our behaviours. So without even noticing it we can get stuck in a negative cycle. This is a thinking trap. Thinking traps, as the name implies, are hard to escape from. If we don't even notice them happening we don't know that we should escape or that any of this background thinking is affecting our mood and keeping us unhappy.

Thinking traps and Negative Automatic Thoughts can snowball – a small negative thought can quickly become a big negative thought.

Let's use the party invitation example again.

You are
invited to a
PARTY

Possible thought:

What will they think of me?
I hope they still like me.

This thought doesn't sound very negative. Maybe it makes us feel a little bit worried and anxious. But if we are low and unhappy it can quickly grow. Let's look at how that might happen – what thoughts might follow the first?

• 'What will they think of me? I hope they still like me.'

• 'What shall I wear?'

• 'I've got nothing to wear!'

• 'I'll feel stupid and ugly.'

• 'I'm not very good at talking to people.'

• 'I'll be really embarrassed and uncomfortable.'

• 'It'll be awful; no one will speak to me.'

• 'They'll think I'm really stupid and ugly.'

• 'They'll be sorry they invited me.'

• 'It'd be better not to go at all.'

• 'That's it; I'm not going.'

- 'If I don't go it just shows how useless I am.'

- 'I'll never make any friends.'

- 'I'll always be lonely.'

- 'Why do I always mess everything up?'

Putting thoughts on trial

Cognitive behaviour therapy takes a close look at thoughts and behaviours. In the previous chapter we examined how your son's or daughter's behaviours might be keeping depression going and considered ways to work with them to increase their activity and break the cycle of depression, inactivity and lack of enjoyment and pleasure.

Now it is time to turn to our thoughts and cognitions and to consider ways of tackling these and turning back the thinking traps that are so common in depression. First, let's review what we have already discussed about thinking and depression.

1. The world is full of information that is not clear.

2. We all use shortcuts to deal with the overload.

3. Shortcuts can lead to thinking traps.

4. If we feel low we are more likely to fall into a negative trap.

5. We probably won't notice that it's a trap.

6. A negative trap will make us feel even worse.

Here's an example of a thinking trap that Emily found herself in. The situation here is that Emily saw her friend Christy talking to the girls who had bullied her.

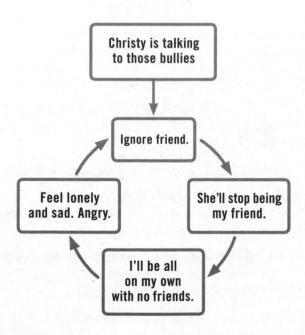

Because Emily saw Christy talking to the girls who had been mean to her, she immediately *thought the worst*. She *assumed* that Christy would stop being her friend. She *imagined* herself with no friends at all. But Emily didn't have any real reason to think these things. She didn't have any evidence that Christy would stop being her friend.

But this thought made her feel even more lonely and sad. She also felt upset with Christy and a bit angry with her. So instead of talking to Christy and being friendly and chatting it over with her as she might have done before, she ignored her. This confused Christy. She didn't realize what Emily was thinking. She had to try to make sense of Emily's behaviour.

It's understandable that Emily thought the worse. But how helpful was it?

Are there other, more helpful thoughts Emily could have had?

Escape the thinking trap

Your son or daughter is likely to be falling into a number of thinking traps. It's likely that they are not aware of these at all. Most of us assume that our thoughts are reasonable and sensible. We tend to accept the judgment that we make. In this section we will highlight how to help your son or daughter to challenge their thoughts. They are likely to need a bit of encouragement and help to do this as well as practice. Don't worry – everyone finds it hard. We just aren't very used to paying attention to our thoughts and so they sneak past us.

There are four stages:

1. Catch the thought – your son or daughter has to be able to 'catch' them before they can do anything with them.

2. Inspect the thought – is there a trap in there? We'll check out a few of the most common thinking traps – it's likely you'll recognize one or two of them.

3. Test the thought – is it reasonable? Or is it just a negative trap?

4. Challenge and replace negative thoughts with more helpful thoughts

Catching thoughts

This is probably the most difficult bit of putting our thoughts on trial. Many thoughts, especially those linked with depression and low mood, are automatic and therefore like habits. Emily's thoughts about Christy were so quick to happen that she didn't even notice them. What she did notice was how sad and lonely she felt. And what she did was to ignore Christy, something that probably made things even worse.

So, how can you help your son or daughter to start to catch their thoughts? Usually it's easiest to start with a specific situation. Something that happened recently is best. It can be helpful to write this down to keep a record of it. Also, writing down situations and thoughts can be a helpful way of standing back from them and getting a bit of distance from them.

If your son or daughter has been keeping an activity log and recording what they did and what their mood was like this could give you some ideas of a specific situation that might be useful. Is there something that happened last week that seemed to make their mood a bit worse? This could be anything but with teenagers it is often something to do with other people or their friends.

On pages 226–7 is a log for writing this down. You might find it helpful to practise this on something in your own life first so that you can get the hang of it before trying to help your son or daughter.

We'll also fill one in as an example. Our example is the party invitation we mentioned before.

What happened (the easy bit)

- Write down what your son or daughter was doing and where they were.
- If it's relevant also add who they were with.

Time and date	What happened	What you thought How much you believe it	Feeling How strong is the feeling?
9.30 a.m. Saturday	Party invitation arrived in post		

Thoughts

These are questions for your child to ask themselves. You might be able to help them with suggestions but beware of answering for them. None of us are mind readers and we can get it wrong when we guess what other people are thinking.

- What went through your mind? What did you say to yourself? What did you 'see' in your mind's eye?
- Write down your thoughts. You might be able to catch more than one – great, put them all down (we've only put down a few to give you the idea).
- How much do you believe each thought?
- Rate the thought(s) from 0 (don't believe it at all) to 100 (completely believe it).

Time and date	What happened	What you thought How much you believe it	Feeling How strong is the feeling?
9.30 a.m. Saturday	Party invitation arrived in post	What will they think of me? I hope they still like me. 50 per cent	
		It'll be awful, no one will speak to me. 70 per cent	

		Why do I always mess everything up? 100 per cent	

Feelings

Now your child considers the effect of their thoughts on their emotions. Again, be available to help them but encourage them to decide for themselves. It might be hard for them so remind them that there isn't a 'right' answer.

- How did that make you feel? Good or bad?

- Can you describe it a bit more? For example, if it was bad, were you sad, worried, angry, upset, irritable or a mixture of these? If you had more than one feeling write them all down.

- How strong was the feeling? Or if you had more than one, how strong was each one?

- Rate the feeing from 0 (nothing at all) to 100 (maximum possible strength).

Time and date	Situation – what happened	What you thought How much you believe it	Feeling How strong is the feeling?
9.30 a.m. Saturday	Party invitation arrived in post	What will they think of me? I hope they still like me. 50 per cent	Worried Anxious 80 per cent
		I'll be awful. No one will speak to me. 70 per cent	Left out Sad 90 per cent
		Why do I always mess everything up? 100 per cent	Useless Depressed 100 per cent

OK, how was that? Can you help your son or daughter to think to more than one example from the last week? Try going back to the activity log for last week. That might include clues to times when they felt low and it might remind them of where they were and what they were doing.

If it is too hard to remember things that happened last week this is not a problem. Your son or daughter can start now by using the next few things that happen that trigger an unhappy, sad, angry, irritable or worried feeling. At this stage don't worry about getting it right or wrong. This is something to practise; they can always try again.

My thought-catching log

Time and date	Situation – what happened	What you thought How much you believe it	Feeling How strong is the feeling?

Checking thoughts

Starting to catch automatic thoughts is the hardest part of checking them and challenging them. We call checking and challenging thoughts putting thoughts on trial. The aim is to inspect the thought and consider how likely it is to be valid, or accurate or helpful. There are a lot of ways we can make mistakes in our thinking.

Thinking mistakes are not always unhelpful. Remember, we described how many people have positive thinking biases – this means we can make positive mistakes as well and they probably make us feel better. For example, (I think) I'm a much better driver than the average driver. But as most people think that they are better than the average driver we can't all be right. So I might be wearing rose-tinted glasses when I think about myself as a driver.

When we make thinking mistakes that keep us feeling unhappy and depressed, or make us feel even worse, or lead to us behaving in ways that make things worse, it's time to catch them, challenge them and chuck them out.

Here are some of the most common thinking traps. We've given a few examples to show how they work. It's likely that your son or daughter (and you) might make a few of them. You might identify some in your son's or daughter's thought-catching log. We've left a space for you to add some examples of your own.

Black and white thinking (or all or nothing thinking)

'I *must* make a good impression at this party or I'll *never* make friends.'

'If I don't get an A in the exam it'll prove how stupid I am.'

....
(Your example)

Over-generalizing

'She's cross with me; I know that she hates me, everyone hates me.'

'If she doesn't invite me to her party I'll *never* make any new friends.'

....
(Your example)

Predicting the worst

'I'm bound to fail that exam. My life will be ruined. I'll never get to college, or get a good job.'

'I'll hate that party; no one will speak to me.'

'She'll stop being my friend.'

....

(Your example)

Self-blaming

'It's because I'm stupid/ugly/horrible/unlovable.'

'I've let everyone down.'

....

(Your example)

Mind reading

'She'll think I'm stupid.'

'They all think I'm ugly.'

'My parents will be so disappointed in me.'

....

(Your example)

Jumping to conclusions

'If I don't get picked for the team I'll be so embarrassed, I won't be able to play again.'

'Where are they? They're late. They're not coming. I've been stood up.'

'They're whispering. I bet they're talking about me.'

....

(Your example)

Challenging thoughts

Putting thoughts on trial

A good starting point is to remember that having a thought doesn't mean that it is true. A thought is just a thought. It could be accurate. It might be completely wrong. It might be partly correct.

Let's look again at Emily's thought:

'She'll stop being my friend.'

Does Emily know this is true? No. Is it inevitable that Christy will stop being her friend? No. Does Emily have much evidence for that thought? Probably not.

How well do your son's or daughter's thoughts stand up to such questioning? Once they have caught their thoughts and put them down on paper you may be able to help them test their thoughts and put them on trial. Some useful questions to consider about the thought include:

- What's the evidence for that thought?
- Do I have enough information to draw that conclusion?
- How could I get more information?
- Is there another way of thinking about that?
- How reasonable was that thought?

- If my best friend had that thought what would I say to them?

- What other thoughts could I have had in the same situation?
- What would my friend (insert name) think if they were in that situation?

To show how that could work let's use the party invitation again. We've seen how one little thought seemed to lead to a whole string of negative thoughts. Let's look at each one of them and see if we can find any thinking errors.

You are invited to a PARTY

What will they think of me?
I hope they still like me.

Thought	Thinking trap
'What will they think of me? I hope they still like me?'	Not too negative – could be neutral. If you go, you'll find out.
'What shall I wear?'	Good question, you could make a plan.
'I've got *nothing* to wear!'	Is that actually true? Is this black-and-white thinking? There's still time to get something new.
'I'll feel stupid and ugly.'	You are predicting the worst. Do you actually *know* what you will feel? Just because you think it doesn't make it true.
'I'm not very good at talking to people.'	Is this true? What evidence do you have? What would your best friend say to you about this? Have there been times when you managed to talk to others? If you are not very good at talking to people is this a skill that you could practise? How do other people who find it difficult to talk to other people manage? Could you practise listening instead?

'I'll be really embarrassed and uncomfortable.'	Sounds like you are predicting the worst again. Do you really know how you will feel in three weeks' time? What other feelings are possible?
'It'll be awful, no one will speak to me.'	Now you are *'awful-izing'* (and yes, we made that word up!). How do you know what will happen at the party? Just because you think something does that make it true? If no one spoke to you what could you do about that?
'They will think I'm really stupid and ugly.'	Will they? How do you know? Are you making the mistake of mind reading?
'They'll be sorry they invited me.'	This is definitely mind reading. Face it, you don't have super powers.
'It'll be better not to go at all.'	Based on what? Is your mind reading, predicting the worst, and black-and-white thinking helping you to make the right decisions? Have you worried about something similar in the past and you found that it turned out OK when you went?

Finding more helpful thoughts

So you have caught your thoughts, had a good look at them, put them on trial and found that many of them are full of traps. What now? Next we replace the automatic thoughts with an alternative thought. We're looking for something that is a bit more neutral, a bit more balanced and a bit more accurate.

Situation: At home, alone, party invitation

Thought	Feeling How strong?	New, more helpful thought	Feeling How strong?
'What will they think of me?' 'I hope they still like me?'	Worried, anxious. 80 per cent	'They wouldn't invite me if they didn't like me.'	Worried, anxious. 60 per cent
		'It might be nice to see them again.'	Pleased. 40 per cent
'I've got nothing to wear.'	Fed up. 70 per cent	'I'll go and check my wardrobe.'	OK 50 per cent
		'I can go and buy something for the party.'	Relieved 80 per cent

'I'll feel stupid and ugly.' 'I'll be really embarrassed and uncomfortable.'	Sad. 80 per cent	'How do I know what I'll feel like?' 'It's too early to know.'	Sad. 60 per cent
'I'm not very good at talking to people.'	Useless. 100 per cent	'Some people do seem better at talking to other people than me.' 'Can I practise talking to people I don't know?'	Useless. 80 per cent Good idea. 60 per cent
'They will think I'm really stupid and ugly.'	Lonely. 90 per cent	'How do I know that's true?' 'They wouldn't invite me if they didn't want to see me.'	Lonely. 10 per cent

Like any thoughts, these new, more helpful thoughts might not always be 'true'. The aim is to find a more balanced thought that is not part of a negative trap. Remember, *all* thoughts are just thoughts. Thoughts are not facts.

It's also important to try to rate your child's feelings again after your son or daughter considers the new, more helpful thought. In the example on the previous page, you'll see that feelings don't necessarily change completely, but overall, they are a little bit less negative. Importantly, the thought-challenging has created some different ideas to consider and some alternative behaviours to try. Your son or daughter might also be able to identify people who can help them try out the behaviours. For example, could a sibling or parent, or friend go with them to buy some new clothes? Could they practise talking at a party with someone they already know? Could you (as their parent) take them to a social situation where they can practise talking to someone they don't know well?

On the next page you'll find a form for your son or daughter to record their own thoughts, feelings and new, more helpful thoughts.

In the following chapter we will look a bit more closely at how to use 'behavioural experiments' to test out thoughts.

Situation _____

Thought	Feeling How strong? 0–100 per cent	New, more helpful thought	Feeling How strong? 0–100 per cent

Dealing with 'stuck thoughts'

Sometimes it's hard to challenge thoughts – some thoughts go round and round in our heads and get stuck. Sometimes we try to work through a problem and go over and over the same thing. This is called **rumination** and it is a common symptom of depression.

It can be hard to recognize when you are stuck in your thinking. This is because we often try to think through our problems and believe that if we just think hard enough we will figure out a way through them. Some kinds of thinking through problems can be useful. We can work out how to avoid problems in the future or take the time to see things from someone else's point of view. This is a way of solving problems. But at other times thinking things over is not helpful and doesn't get us anywhere. A specific kind of rumination is called **brooding**. Thinking about what went wrong in the past and focusing on what has already happened can become brooding and may make you feel worse. It can get in the way of actually changing and finding new ways to solve problems.

The following types of question that we sometimes ask ourselves can indicate that we are ruminating, rather than actively problem-solving.

- 'Why on earth did I do it that way?'
- 'Would it have made any difference if I'd done it differently?'
- 'How did I get myself into that situation?'
- 'I should have said "............". Then if they said "..........", maybe that would have worked.'

- 'Why does this kind of thing always happen to me?'
- 'What have I done wrong?'
- 'Is it something about the kind of person I am?'
- 'Do I deserve to have bad things happen to me?'

This kind of stuck thinking does not help improve low mood or depression. It does feel helpful so it can be hard to give it up. If your son or daughter tends to ruminate and get stuck here are some ways to help them stop ruminating and start getting on with life.

1. Distraction

This is so simple it's hard to believe it can work. But really, it can.

You've almost certainly used distraction with your children when they were younger to avoid tantrums or to break up an argument between siblings. It is still a useful tactic for teenagers and adults who are getting stuck in rumination.

Distraction can be immediate and short term. You might be able to attract their attention onto something else happening right now.

- Exercise is good. If your son or daughter is putting effort into running, cycling, dance, an aerobics class or a game of football they can't pay attention to 'stuck' thoughts at the same time.
- Encourage them to watch a film, play music, read a novel.

If they can face it a funny film is a great distraction from rumination.

- Persuade them to do something practical. This is also good if it's helping someone else. For example, cooking dinner for the family, making a cake, hanging out some washing, cleaning the bathroom, or playing with younger brothers or sisters can all be good distractions.
- They could play a challenging computer game.
- They could learn how to knit or sew or do DIY.
- Your child could visit a sick or elderly relative or neighbour. Taking an interest in other people's difficulties can force attention away from the self and on to others.

2. Try problem solving

We have included information about problem solving in the next chapter. This is a much more constructive approach than rumination and quite different. See if your son or daughter can use the methods of problem solving to deal with their stuck thoughts.

3. Learn to let negative thoughts 'go'

This is a different way to deal with stuck thoughts. Remember, thoughts are just thoughts. They come and go, in and out of the mind. Some are positive and some are negative. Thoughts are not facts. Thoughts themselves are not real even if they are about things that were real. Much of the time we don't even notice our thoughts so we know that they can come and go. Many young people and parents will have heard about **Mindfulness** – your son or daughter may even have learned about Mindfulness at school. If they are interested in learning more about Mindfulness this can help manage repetitive negative thoughts – it is also a useful life skill and something that family members can learn together and practise together.

Often thoughts that get stuck are about things that happened in the past. It can be a long time ago or something that happened earlier today. Things in the past can't be changed. We can learn from the past and this is important. But going over and over the same event in the past is probably not learning. Bad memories and thoughts can be caught up with a lot of difficult feelings like anger and rage, loss and failure. If this is the case for your son or daughter, those memories and the experiences that went with them are part of who they are. But they are only a part of who they are. Their past experiences do not define who your son or daughter is now, or what they can become. This is why accepting the past and focusing on what is happening now and in the future can be a much more creative way forward.

Stuck thoughts can also include a lot of self-blame. Your teenager may have a critical inner voice pointing out all their flaws and failings, reminding them of the errors they have made and highlighting all their weaknesses. If your son or daughter is their own worst critic they may find a new psychological approach – **Self-compassion** – useful. You and your son or daughter can read more about self-compassion here:

www.compassionatemind.co.uk/

Other ways to escape from stuck thinking

1. Writing about bad experiences can help deal with the jumbled-up thoughts and feelings. It's not important to write down everything completely or perfectly. Just getting thoughts down on paper can introduce a bit of distance. Better still, take the paper and lock it away in a drawer to increase the sense of distance. No one else needs to read it or comment or judge it – this is just for your son or daughter.

2. Allocate a specific 'worry time' each day. Thirty minutes is plenty long enough. Make sure that your son or daughter is busy immediately before and after the 'worry time' so that they are forced to stop when the time is up. If worries and stuck thoughts start outside of this time they know they can put them aside and come back to them later.

3. Intrusive negative thoughts can be more distressing if they are kept inside. Your son or daughter may find it helpful to share them with someone else. It doesn't need to be you – in fact, it might be better if it was not you. Is there another adult (teacher, sports coach, aunt/uncle) they get on well with? Or what about a telephone or online service for teenagers? Our resources include contact details for online and telephone support services which are specifically for young people.

4. Join a group to learn Mindfulness meditation. Many schools and local groups now teach Mindfulness. Your GP might be able to refer your son or daughter to a class. You might be able to learn with them and practise together.

9

Helping your child to get the facts and to solve problems

It is human nature to constantly think about things, to remember past events, to think about what will happen in the future and to try to solve issues that haven't even happened yet. We all think all the time, every moment of the day. While this can be a fantastic thing because it means we can be incredibly creative and successful as individuals and as a species, it can also have some downsides.

As you'll remember from Chapters 6 and 8, our thinking has a direct influence on how we feel. When we become stuck in unhelpful thinking cycles, this can produce very unpleasant emotions such as distress, anxiety, worry, depression and rage, just to name a few. These emotional reactions can be rational and useful at times. For example, if you walked out of your house in the morning to find that your shed had been broken into and some of your expensive tools had been stolen you might feel very angry. You might think it is very unfair that someone has just invaded your property in this way. This might lead you to report the crime to your local police and they may work with you to help with safety measures in your neighbourhood and possibly with finding your tools. In this situation you are thinking about and responding to the FACTS of what has happened. The facts are that unfortunately some of your possessions have been damaged and stolen.

When we are depressed or very anxious, we often don't operate on the basis of facts. You may remember from the previous chapter that people make many thinking errors when they are depressed. Their thinking is biased and it's as if they are wearing depression goggles where only the negative things get through the goggles and the rest of the information gets filtered out. When we are depressed we start to believe our thoughts without looking around at the other information available to us. This can lead to the unhelpful belief that 'If I *think* something therefore it must be true'.

Depressed and anxious individuals also respond on the basis of their feelings. I feel (e.g. anxious, horrible, hopeless, awful, sad) therefore this must mean that's how it is. Our thoughts and feelings can be a powerful source of information for different situations but sometimes we tend to forget that these indicators are often inaccurate and sometimes not based on the facts at all.

Getting more facts

Hopefully you have managed to read through the ideas in Chapter 8 about how to help your child think differently, and in a more balanced way, in order to feel differently. This is achieved by looking at the facts of the situation (rather than completely depending on what the thoughts or feelings are saying). Sometimes we find that simply working through thoughts in this way is not enough. We find that we need more information and facts before we can come to a confident conclusion about any given situation.

For example, someone hearing the sound of breaking glass in their garden at night may quickly jump to the conclusion that their shed has been broken into and their tools are being stolen. This thought may produce fear and anger. They may be able to do some balanced thinking about it. They might be able to imagine a number of alternative explanations.

So they may consider the possibility that the sound was not breaking glass but the neighbours clearing up bottles from their party the night before. They may also think that perhaps the foxes are getting into the bins again and the sound was one of the bins falling over. These interpretations may help the person to feel less fear and anger in the situation and allow them to step away from their emotions for long enough to consider different alternatives. However, they will certainly need more facts before they can confirm which is the most accurate way of thinking about this situation. They might choose to gather the facts by getting their partner up to check the garden and shed with them for the evidence.

When people have depression, often they don't check the facts in relation to the different situations they find themselves in. Rather, they rely much more on what their thoughts are telling them and what their feelings are suggesting.

'I think this, therefore it must be right.' (e.g. 'I'm useless at everything.')

'I feel this way, therefore that's how it is.' (e.g. 'I feel hopeless therefore there's no point in trying anything.')

Hopefully you can recognize that this is not necessarily a good way of making decisions. Often the information given by thoughts and feelings is misleading. What is much more helpful is to get into the habit of gathering the facts about a situation. There are usually one of two outcomes as a result of gathering the facts:

1. You find that the facts don't match up with the thoughts and feelings and therefore this provides more convincing information to help with alternative and balanced thinking (e.g. It was the neighbours, after all, who were making the noise).

or

2. You find that the facts do match your thoughts and feelings and then you usually need to find a way of facing up to, coping and doing something about the situation (e.g. the shed has been broken into and therefore the police need to be called and the rest of the items need to be secured in some way in the meantime).

This chapter is all about helping your child to gather the FACTS – fact finding, and helping them to face up to and cope with situations – problem solving.

Fact finding

We suggest that fact finding works best when you approach it in a planned, systematic way, a bit like a scientist would if he or she were trying to put a new theory or substance to the test. Of course it is best done together with your child so we encourage you to talk to them about your ideas or, better still, get them to come up with some of their own ideas. The following are guidelines for designing and carrying out fact finders:

1. Write down the **thoughts or beliefs** that you want to test.

2. Next write down an idea for the **fact finder** to test these out.

3. Then write down your child's **prediction** about what you think is going to happen when you do the test.

4. Then you or your child **carries it out**.

5. Next, note down **what actually happened** and **whether the prediction was right**.

6. Finally, whatever the outcome, it's helpful to have a think about **what the outcome means** in relation to the thought(s) being tested. Is there a more **balanced view** based on the information?

7. **What's next?** Sometimes doing one fact finder leads to ideas for other things that can be put to the test. It's worth putting some ideas together about further fact finders.

Example:

Lin was convinced that girls in her class were talking about her behind her back and she saw them giggling a few times at school, and when she saw them at the shopping mall. She believed that the girls thought she was weird and they didn't like her.

1. Thought(s) to test

The girls in my class don't like me and they think I'm weird

2. Fact finder

Lin and her mother talked about the various ways that Lin could get some more facts about this situation. They considered Lin speaking with some other girls who were friendlier to see what they had noticed. They also talked about Lin saying hello to the girls the next time she walked past them. Lin's mum suggested that Lin invites them over for dinner after school but Lin thought this was a terrible idea and refused to do this. Finally, they decided that Lin was going to ask one of the girls if she could borrow a pen during class and she would say 'Hi' or smile at one of the other girls next time she walked past. This was very hard for Lin but she could see that it made sense to see how the girls would respond in order to get some more information and facts.

3. Predictions

Lin predicted that the girls would either ignore her or that they would tell her to leave them alone.

4. Carry it out

It took Lin quite a while to get enough courage to do this Fact Finder. Her mum didn't put pressure on her but she did carry on encouraging her and then also suggested some sort of nice treat for Lin if she managed to do it, no matter what the outcome. Lin suggested that she'd love to get her nails done so it was agreed that they would both go and get their nails done once Lin carried the tasks out.

5. What actually happened?

Lin finally asked one of the girls if she could borrow a pen in maths because she was sitting right behind her. The girl smiled and said she didn't have a spare pen but she could borrow one of her pencils. Lin thanked her and smiled back. At the end of the class Lin gave the pencil back and the girl told her to hold onto it for the day and to give it back to her tomorrow.

This gave Lin the courage to say hello to one of the other girls when she walked past. The girl said hi back and her friend then turned around and told Lin to remember to bring back the pencil tomorrow in a humorous sort of way. Lin said she would and laughed.

Was the prediction right?

No, neither of Lin's predictions were correct.

6. What does it all mean?

Perhaps these girls don't dislike Lin at all, or think she's weird, they just don't know her yet.

Is there a balanced view?

Lin and her mum talked about what happened and Lin decided that her more balanced view went something like this:

'I'm still new so these girls don't know me yet. The fact that they seemed friendly means that they might think I'm all right or at least they don't dislike me.'

7. What's next?

Lin decided to carry on being friendly to these girls to see what happens. It might lead to nothing but it might mean she will get to know more people in the school. She decided to have a short conversation with the girl who lent her the pencil.

My Child's fact finder

Thought(s) to test
Fact finder
Prediction
Do it

So what happened?

Was the prediction right?

What does it all mean?

Is there a balanced view?

What's next?

Problem solving

As described above, sometimes after we have gathered all the facts we find that our predictions, thoughts and beliefs about a particular situation are not true. Sometimes the opposite happens. We find out that our predictions and thoughts are true and are based on reality.

While finding out about this can be difficult at first, it's much better to know this rather than carry on guessing and turning things over and over in our minds without knowing the truth. Getting to this point provides a really good opportunity to face up to the situation and do something about it. You may remember that young people with depression can all too easily become caught up in unhelpful cycles of negative thinking and avoidance of situations – this is called **rumination**. Rumination prevents them from facing up to things that perhaps need to be dealt with and solved. While it is easier to hide away and avoid things, rumination and avoidance severely reduce a young person's confidence and provide further opportunities for negative thinking, which in turn feeds depression.

How we see problems

Everyone encounters problems much of the time, from small daily situations such as finding the time to juggle competing demands to much bigger issues that may affect the whole family or our future. The way we approach problems is very important.

If we see problems as terrible, as a nuisance, there to ruin our lives, or as overwhelming and unmanageable, this will not motivate us to try to solve them and we will tend to avoid facing up to things. If we see problems in a slightly different way, we will be much more inclined to be proactive and to work to find solutions.

It may be helpful for you to have a think right now about your child's general approach towards problems. Do they tend to see problems as an opportunity to find solutions and to learn something or do they tend to view problems as overwhelming and to be avoided at all costs? Are there ways that you can encourage them to approach situations more and to have a more positive attitude towards problems and solving them?

Initially you may choose to simply do this through example and you may be doing this already. Perhaps talking with them about a fairly simple situation that you have managed to overcome or solve is a good place to start. Obviously you'll need to choose appropriate situations and topics to discuss with your child but don't underestimate the power of modelling. Your child will be picking up tips and ideas from you when you don't even think they are listening or even when you don't think they are interested in what you are saying! In addition, as we have mentioned before, parents are excellent models for their children and your son or daughter is learning from you all the time. If you model (i.e. do) active problem solving when you are in a tricky situation they are much more likely to try this approach themselves.

Rumination is not the same as problem solving

With any type of problem solving, we do need to think about the problem we are facing and there also needs to be some thinking time devoted to making up and generating possible solutions. However, sometimes people get stuck on the thinking part and then forget to move onto the doing part. So they might dwell on their problem and turn it over and over in their mind. They might come up with all sorts of different solutions but then also get stuck on turning these over and over in their minds. This is another example of rumination. When it goes on for too long it becomes very unhelpful and can contribute to negative feelings such as depression and anxiety.

In rumination mode people get stuck with asking all the WHY questions:

- Why is this happening?
- Why can't things be different?
- Why me?
- Why do I always mess everything up?
- Why on earth did I say such a stupid thing?

To move into problem-solving mode it's much more helpful to ask more HOW questions:

- How are we going to overcome this?
- How can I approach this?
- How can I get help with this problem?
- How have I managed this before?
- How would my friend deal with this situation?

These types of question make it more likely that the issue is dealt with, rather than just thought about. Many people are excellent problem solvers in their minds, or even on paper, and they can ask lots of useful HOW questions. That is, they can come up with some very helpful ideas about how to overcome different problems.

The next hurdle sometimes is about then putting these ideas to action. This is quite an important point because having a brilliant list of solutions won't change the situation **on its own**. It might make the person feel better for a while because they have some ideas but these ideas then need to be applied in the real world. Sometimes people get stuck here because they feel their solutions won't work very well, or they keep looking for the perfect solution, or the one that they feel very confident about. The best method is to pick one or a couple of solutions that seem OK compared to the others and then to try them out. There is usually nothing to lose and a lot to learn. If the solutions don't prove to be helpful then it's time to go back to the list and find some others to try out.

Encouraging your child to solve problems

If you feel that your child could be applying problem solving more often in order to help them feel more in control, more confident and more engaged in life's decisions and situations, then see below for a step-by-step guide to this technique. Sometimes simply starting with something very simple and minor can give a person a sense of motivation and confidence and it can counteract those very unhelpful thoughts such as 'it's all hopeless', I'm useless', 'it's no good', 'there's nothing I can do', 'it will be awful' and so on.

When you tackle a problem head-on, find some solutions, put them into action and find some sort of resolution, it's pretty hard to think these sorts of thoughts with quite as much confidence. Instead, young people who engage in problem solving on a regular basis are more likely to have thoughts along the lines of 'I can cope', 'everything has a solution', 'it will be OK', 'there's hope still', 'I can look after myself' etc. These thinking styles will have a positive effect on mood and build more confidence.

Feel free to show this chapter to your child or simply encourage them to apply these strategies in your own way. It usually works best to write each step down.

Solving problems – step by step

This skill has particular steps that are best taken in the right order.

STEP 1 Decide on what the problem is – **name it**:

'The problem is _____

_____

_____,'

(Remember that attitude towards problems is important at this stage so this is a good time to see the problem as an opportunity rather than a nuisance.)

STEP 2 Come up with some possible solutions – it's helpful to let your imagination run wild for a while and to note down some funny and ridiculous solutions. Keeping the humour in this helps some people to come up with more solutions and to be creative with it.

STEP 3 Think about each solution and how good you think it is – will it solve the problem completely or maybe even just a little?

STEP 4 Choose one or two of your favourite solutions – they don't have to be perfect, in fact most of the time solutions are not perfect, they're just OK.

STEP 5 Plan how and when you will try them out.

STEP 6 Try them. Did they work?

STEP 7 If not, try some other ones.

STEP 8 Stop and remind yourself that it's great you have remembered to practise solving problems, no matter what the outcome.

Emily's stepdad wanted to talk to Emily about how she was getting on at school because he was concerned about how upset she sometimes looked in the mornings before catching the school bus. He had a suspicion that Emily was having some problems with her friendships because she had mentioned some things about it a few times so he picked a time when she was downstairs and looked fairly relaxed to speak with her. He simply began by asking 'How's school?' Emily scrunched her face and shrugged. Chris could tell things weren't great. He asked whether there were some problems with friends or the other students. Emily shrugged again and then Chris fell silent for quite some time and they both stared at the TV.

Chris thought that was the end of the conversation but to his surprise after some time Emily spoke up and said that there were some bullies on the bus and at school and she didn't know what to do about it. She said that she really wished these girls would like her but instead they said nasty things and sometimes took her things. She said one of the girls also once took her folder and threw it out of the bus window. Chris was quite alarmed to hear this but he kept his feelings to himself. He told Emily that he was really glad she had told him about this and it sounded like a big problem that needed to be tackled, and he added that every problem always has a solution. Emily told him that she didn't want to do anything because she didn't want to make it worse and she didn't want to ruin the chances of these girls liking her in the future.

Chris acknowledged that this was tricky and he grabbed a pen and notepad and started to make some notes. Emily looked curious so he asked her whether they could jot some ideas down about this together. Emily shrugged (which Chris was beginning to understand as an 'OK, I don't mind' response from Emily). He jotted down the problem and then tried to help Emily come up with some ideas for solutions. They came up with a couple but were interrupted because dinner was ready. During dinner Emily came up with a couple more and Chris suggested a few ridiculous ideas to make Emily laugh (which she did, thankfully). They returned to the task after dinner, while putting the dishes away.

The notes Chris and Emily made looked like this:

The problem is: Emily is being bullied, which is making her very upset, and she doesn't want to make things worse.

Possible solutions:

1. Leave it, don't do anything.

2. Stop catching the bus to school.

3. Change schools.

4. Never go to school again.

5. Tell the bullies to stop it.

6. Talk to the teachers.

7. Ignore the bullies completely.

8. Get Mum or Dad to talk to the teachers.

9. Get Mum to call one of the girls' mothers.

10. Cast a magic spell that stops these girls from being able to speak.

11. Get friends to help.

How good are these solutions at solving the problem?

1. Nothing will change if I don't do anything.

2. Could get a lift with Mum but the bullies will still be at school.

3. Not really that easy, plus I would miss my friends and the teachers are OK.

4. Sounds great, but I would miss out on lots of things in the future and it would be pretty boring.

5. They won't listen and it might get worse.

6. They might help but the bullies could get really angry.

7. This would be so hard. It might put them off a bit.

8. This would be a bit like number 6.

9. This could help a bit, but it would have to be in a way that wouldn't get the bullies in trouble.

10. This would be brilliant, if only we had a magic wand!

11. They might have some ideas about how to help.

Favourite solutions:

Ignore the bullies completely

Get Mum to call one of the other mums

Talk to friends about it

How and when to try solutions:

Start ignoring them completely from tomorrow and see what happens. Tell Mum the plan and ask her to call this week. Tell her how important it is that this girl doesn't get in too much trouble. Talk to friends about it to see if they have any other ideas (talk to one friend on the phone tonight and the other tomorrow at school).

Result:

After a week of completely ignoring the bullies Emily found that they were not giving her such a hard time any more. Emily's mum called one of the other mums and had a friendly chat about 'some problems' between their daughters. The mum said that she would have a chat with her daughter about it and hopefully Emily and her daughter will be able to sort out their difficulties. Emily also talked to her friends about it. Their opinion was that these girls were really not very nice and they couldn't understand why Emily cared what they thought. They advised her to keep ignoring them and to tell the teachers if they ever took anything else of hers. Emily felt better after this because she started to think that maybe she didn't want these girls to like her after all and maybe she could care less about it, a bit like her friends.

Is the problem still there? What else can we try?:

The problem certainly got better after a couple of weeks. It's not completely solved because the girls still sometimes huddle together on the bus and look as though they are talking about Emily. This makes Emily feel uncomfortable for a while but then she reminds herself of her other friends and the fact that she doesn't really want to be friends with people who treat others in this way. Emily also now puts on headphones and listens to her favourite music while on the bus.

Chris regularly checked with Emily about how the plan was going. He asked her how she felt about it. Emily said that she felt a bit better because she felt a bit more like she was doing something about it. He told her that it was fantastic she was facing up to this and working it out. He encouraged Emily to always come and talk to him or her mother if anything else was bothering her or if she wanted to find some help with finding solutions.

If you wish to apply this strategy with your child for any problems that he or she may be experiencing you can find a blank problem-solving worksheet on the following pages.

My child's problem solving

STEP 1 Name it:

The problem is

_____

_____

_____

_____

_____

STEP 2 Come up with some possible solutions – go on, add some funny and ridiculous ones too, it helps with imagination.

_____

_____

_____

_____

_____

_____

STEP 3 Have a think about each solution and how good you think it is – will it solve the problem completely or maybe even just a little?

_____

_____

_____

_____

_____

STEP 4 Choose one or two of your favourite solutions – they don't have to be perfect. In fact, most of the time solutions are not perfect, they're just OK.

My favourite solutions are

_____

_____

_____

_____

_____

_____

STEP 5 Plan how and when you will try them out.

_____

_____

_____

_____

_____

_____

STEP 6 Try them. Did they work?

_____

_____

_____

_____

_____

_____

STEP 7 If not, try some other ones – which ones will you try next? Do you need to think of some extra solutions?

_____

_____

_____

_____

_____

_____

STEP 8 Stop and remind yourself that it's great you have remembered to practise solving problems, no matter what the outcome.

How do you feel now?

_____

_____

_____

_____

_____

_____

Part 4

Additional strategies to try

10

Stress levels and family communications

Keeping stress levels as low as possible

Depression can get worse when there are high levels of external demands, pressures and changes in the family that cause stress. Of course this is not surprising since too much pressure and stress can make a person feel more anxious and overwhelmed and therefore affect mood in a negative way.

There are different forms of stress. Some forms of stress for a teenager come from the pressures of schoolwork, exams, and wanting to do well academically. Other stresses may originate from peers and friends. Often at this age relationships with friends and boyfriends/girlfriends can be intense and change-able. There is a lot to be dealing with in terms of 'fitting in' while at the same time trying to find your own identity and confidence as an individual.

Considering the impact of social media

With the additional various messages about who to be friends with, what to wear, how to behave, what to own, and where to go coming from the media and social media sites, today's teenager is regularly bombarded with potential stressors. The more vulnerable young person may see these messages as additional evidence that they are somehow 'not good enough' compared with others. While the speed of communication and various social media possibilities in the modern world can be wonderful, and allows us to do some amazing things, it can also be an additional stick for the young, depressed person to beat themselves with.

Of course for others social media is a way of maintaining contact with peers when otherwise it would be too difficult for various reasons (e.g. feeling too low to go out, but still keeping in contact with good friends). Social media sites can provide excellent sources of support and advice to young people (and their parents) who would otherwise feel isolated and alone. However, your son or daughter may need help to find their way to supportive and safe sites and contacts via social media and this is an important issue to talk about with them.

Parent reflections:

'Perhaps encourage your child to delete Facebook if it upsets them. Really, you don't need it. People create a narrative for the life they want the world to see. If you are lonely in your bedroom feeling fat and all you see are air-brushed "friends"

274

on Facebook, really you need to delete the thing for a while and see real people! When you have real friends who you see on a regular basis, you see them warts and all, don't you? You have to be well and established in your life to survive this odd slant on it. Yet at the same time you don't want your child to miss out. Yet seeing your friends on Facebook apparently partying without you turns the negative thinking switch on very easily.'

There is only so much you can do as parents to help reduce your child's stresses in the realm of school and friends/peers. We have already given you ideas about how you can help your child to think differently, respond differently, test things out and to problem-solve tricky situations. Sometimes it is appropriate or necessary to become more involved with your child's school when there are issues such as bullying or academic difficulties. You may also feel that too much time on social media sites is having a detrimental effect on your child's mental health. It is advisable to keep a close eye on this. A young person who is struggling with depression may become more depressed if insensitive friends are regularly posting messages to show how much fun they are having without them. If these sites are negatively influencing your child's mood, it may be a good idea to suggest a break from them for a specific length of time. You may be able to negotiate this for several days to begin with and then review with your child whether it has made them feel any differently. Why not approach this as an experiment? Something to try out for a few days and find out about, rather than as an outright ban.

Time management

Although this point may sound somewhat contrary to what we have suggested in Chapter 7, sometimes stress can come from having too much to do. As explained in Chapter 7, we recommend that you help your child to engage in meaningful, enjoyable activities in order to lift their mood. Often young people who have depression have withdrawn from previous activities that they enjoyed and it is important to encourage them to return to these. There are, however, some young people who seem to be going from one activity to the next, but who are still feeling depressed a lot of the time. There may be several things that are happening in this kind of situation.

One of these may be related to the level of engagement in the activity. Young people may be doing something, such as going to a sports club, but may not actually be immersing themselves in the activity in a meaningful way. Their mind may still be turning over many negative things or they may be regularly judging their performance in a negative way, or perhaps comparing themselves too much to others. In this situation the chapter on changing unhelpful thoughts would be very useful (Chapter 8).

Another possibility is that the young person is simply doing too much or the constant activities are a way of avoiding facing their depressed feelings head-on. When constant activities start to feel like avoidance or a chore and something to get through rather than something to enjoy, this begins to increase the stress and pressure on the young person. It is not uncommon, for example, for some families to struggle with attendance at treatment appointments simply because the young person has so many after-school activities and so much homework that there isn't any spare time left. Reducing a young person's commitments may sometimes be helpful when too many activities are causing stress and leaving no time for quiet relaxation and to work on their depression.

Relationships in the family

Despite your support and encouragement, it will be likely that there is a limit to how much influence you will be able to have on your teenager's world outside of the home. This is fine for the most part and part of growing up for every young person. You may, however, have more influence on what is going on at home. Some forms of stress for a young person may be influenced by relationships. If this is the case for your child then this is something that might be more within your control. Have a think for a moment about how well people are getting along in the family. Are there a lot of arguments? Do family members often end up misunderstanding what others are trying to say or what they mean? Does your child express anger or irritability when speaking to others in the family? Are there topics that always seem to lead to arguments? You may be able to identify opportunities for reducing these types of stressful situation within the family home.

If this is relevant to your family then it may be helpful to read some of the suggestions in this chapter. You may already have ideas of your own that you could put into action. Sometimes just taking time to think about such issues can lead to a whole range of thoughts and ideas worth trying. Reducing stress in the home can be another piece of the puzzle in reducing your child's depression. And the more pieces you have, the greater the chances of success. You might want to discuss these ideas with your child. What are their views about how people are getting along in the home? Do they recognize any relationship difficulties that then cause them to feel stressed, angry, irritable or low? What ideas do they have about helping people to get along more? Is there anything they could be doing differently to change this for the better?

Promoting good communication and avoiding conflict

Communication with teenagers at the best of times can be challenging. When a teenager is depressed it can become even more difficult. You may recall the biases in thinking when someone is depressed; it becomes much more likely that the depressed person hears the things that are said to them in negative ways. This increases the likelihood of communication problems and conflict. There is research that shows conflict with family members is higher for depressed teenagers compared with teenagers who are not depressed. There are also suggestions by studies that family conflict may have a further negative effect on the teenager's depressed mood. It's understandable that when a member of the family has depression, it often puts a lot of strain on family relationships and therefore the likelihood for conflict is much higher.

Below are some examples of how depression can twist what young people hear and interpret from what others say. It is not something that people tend to think about when they are communicating with people who are depressed. It is also not something that depressed young people are consciously aware of if they haven't been taught about the thinking errors in depression.

You say:	They hear:
'Why are you in your room again?'	'You're no fun, why can't you be different?'
'Pick up this mess.'	'You can't do anything right.'
'Help me with dinner.'	'You never help around here.'
'Have you done your homework?'	'You haven't done what you're supposed to again.'
'You haven't seen your friends this week.'	'You're not trying hard enough.'
'You used to like playing netball.'	'You're hopeless, you can't even play netball any more.'
'What's wrong?'	'There's something wrong with you.'
'I like that dress.'	'I hate the other dresses.'

Can you think of any recent examples when you said something or asked your child something and the reaction was completely over the top and out of line with the conversation topic or request? If you can, then chances are that their depression twisted your words and your child actually heard this and interpreted it in an unrealistically negative way. This is not your fault or theirs. Depression has a sneaky way of doing this regularly. Keeping this in mind may help you to prepare for these types of thinking errors and to respond in a calm and thoughtful way.

Robert's mum says something along the lines of 'Robert, could you please clean your room this weekend, it's a mess'. This would seem like a reasonable request, especially if Robert's mum has had a busy week at work and Robert's room has been a mess for some time. Robert may hear this in a much more negative way such as 'You never do what you are supposed to. You can't even keep your room clean. You are nothing but trouble.'

This is most certainly not the message that Robert's mum was giving but depression has a way of twisting things so that they fit in with the person's current view of him or herself. In Robert's case, he currently views himself as a failure and no good. You can see how this could easily lead to misunderstandings between Robert and his mum and even to conflict and arguments. Robert might become angry and irritable as a result of his thoughts about the request and he may respond either in an aggressive way (e.g. telling his mum to stop being on his back all the time) or he might withdraw even further (e.g. stay in his room and just watch television or go out without telling his mum where he is going or when he will be back).

Robert's mum may find this quite confusing and frustrating and she may respond with irritability as well, or she may take a more passive approach of 'what's the use?' Communication difficulties such as these may reinforce Robert's already negative views of himself and his life (e.g. 'I can't get along with anyone', 'no one cares').

When trying to avoid or reduce communication problems and conflict we suggest you keep the following points in mind:

- Spend more time talking to your child about positive, humorous or neutral things at appropriate times (to model and encourage better and more frequent communication in general – you may not get the response you want but giving a consistent and clear message that you want to communicate regularly can be very helpful).

- If you know certain topics often lead to arguments (e.g. helping more around the house, using the computer, getting to school on time) ask yourself whether it is absolutely necessary to bring these things up now.
- Think about the timing of your requests. If you know that your child is in a bad mood or has had a bad day at school, delay the request until they seem to be more relaxed.
- When making requests, try to always keep your child's depressed way of thinking in mind – how might he or she hear this, how might depression twist what you're trying to say?
- Take some time and think beforehand about what you want to communicate and what you need to say in order for this to be heard in the way you want it to.
- Give clear instructions with a clear rationale to avoid misunderstandings (e.g. 'I'd really like to clean the house a bit this weekend and I need some help. Since you know where most of your things go in your room, and you cleaned it well last time, could you give that a tidy and this will leave less for me to do? I can do the hoovering bit if you want').
- If you feel yourself becoming irritated, frustrated or angry, take a moment out of the situation. In this quiet moment ask yourself whether your child is responding in ways that fit with a depressed way of thinking. Decide on the best course of action depending on your evaluation (e.g. change communication style, delay it for a while, give a rationale).
- Give choices in order to hand over more responsibility for resolving conflict and improving communication (e.g. 'We need to talk about this difficulty and see if we can solve

it, would you rather talk about it this evening or on the weekend when we have more time?').

- Use problem solving strategies (Chapter 9) to work on communication issues together as a family.
- Draw up schedules or contracts in order to establish ground rules or to ensure everyone keeps to previously agreed points (this can be something to refer back to in times of disagreement). Stick this on the fridge. (Example: 'Mum and Dad have agreed not to remind me about homework for a week. I have agreed to come down for dinner every day this week'.)

Robert's mum asked Robert if they could talk about some things that were on her mind about the house. She asked Robert to choose a good time to do this. Robert seemed quite uninterested but said he didn't mind if they talked on Saturday morning about it since he wasn't doing anything then. Robert's mum agreed and she reminded him about it on Saturday morning.

She told Robert that she was struggling with keeping the house clean and having two jobs and wondered whether he had any solutions for this. Robert suggested that they get a cleaner but they both laughed because this was out of the question at the moment because of a lack of money. He knew what she was getting at and so he said that he could help out a bit more but that his sister needed to pull her weight too. Robert's mum agreed. They spent a bit of time talking about what would be possible. Robert agreed to work on his room being a bit tidier and he said he would feed and clean up after the pets and do his own washing.

Robert's mum said that this would make a big difference and it was agreed that a schedule would be drawn up, which included his sister, and hung on the fridge. Robert's mum suggested that if they could all keep to the schedule for a couple of weeks it would be good to have a treat as a reward and maybe have a barbecue. Robert said he'd rather have a 'cinema night' at home (something they used to do).

11

Expectations and positive reinforcement

Keeping expectations realistic

Many young people (and adults) who experience depression tend to also hold quite high expectations of themselves and sometimes of others. This is an interesting finding when you consider the types of negative thoughts and beliefs that people have when they are depressed. Common thinking patterns include judgments about failure, having to be a certain way, or even having to be perfect, blaming yourself for many things, and having to measure up to others. It is not entirely clear whether being depressed leads to these kinds of thoughts and beliefs or whether they were part of the individual's personality before and then become more pronounced with the onset of depression. Whatever the order of events, it is useful to reflect on whether this is an issue for your child.

We suggest that young people and families would benefit from being on the lookout for overly high expectations. For example, a teenager may be struggling with low mood and at the same time be expecting to achieve very high marks in school, which is what he or she may normally be used to. Having motivation for good marks is positive but it may also be unrealistic to expect such high achievements in the present circumstances. You may recall that some of the symptoms of depression affect a young person's ability to sleep well, to have energy, to concentrate and to make decisions. The depression symptoms may therefore have a temporary effect on how a young person copes with school demands, as well as other daily demands.

Keeping your child's expectations in mind can be useful and it might be a matter of providing regular reminders when you spot overly high expectations creeping in.

Lin comes home from school very disappointed that she only got a pass mark on her most recent maths test. Lin's mum notices that she is putting pressure on herself again and tries to remind her about a more realistic viewpoint:

'Your mood has been quite low this week so it's great that you've managed to go to school every day and keep on top of your homework. I know you're used to getting very good marks but right now you are doing the best you can and that's good enough. Besides, your teachers know you are having some difficulties with your mood so they will understand.'

This type of response models to Lin that it is OK not to expect too much from herself while she is dealing with depression. It challenges the typical 'I'm a failure', 'nothing is working out' and 'I'm not good enough' depressive thoughts. This response encourages thoughts along the lines of 'I'm doing an OK job', 'I don't have to be perfect', 'I'm fine the way I am', 'It's good enough'.

While you are on the lookout for your child's unrealistic expectations you will naturally also notice times when your, your partner's or other family members' expectations become overly high and unrealistic. It can be a very tricky task to balance both encouraging your child to participate in things and at the same time not overloading them with too many demands and expectations. There is no right way for everyone. We simply suggest it may be helpful to be mindful of your child's depression symptoms and how these may be impacting on their ability to function currently. For example, your child may be experiencing increased tiredness due to the depression and may therefore find it more difficult to keep as active as they were previously. They may also be having sleeping problems or concentration difficulties that are impacting on things like being able to remember things (e.g. remembering to do the

287

chores and remembering what the homework is that week) and being able to focus on work in class or on reading.

Positive reinforcement

While keeping an eye on keeping expectations realistic, it is also a good idea to help young people notice their achievements and progress. We all tend to respond well to positive reinforcement on a regular basis. Recall the last time your boss at work mentioned to you that you did something well, or the last time a friend of yours commented on something you were wearing or doing in a positive way.

Chances are that these instances made you feel good and encouraged you to do more of the same. This is a natural human response. Let's face it, most of us wouldn't go to work if we didn't receive the ultimate positive reinforcement of our pay at the end of the month! Positive reinforcement is something that parents naturally use when their children are younger. For example, a parent may notice that their toddler is trying to stand in order to reach for a toy. The parent may smile and make encouraging noises or say positive encouraging things to the toddler to show their delight and support. The toddler may respond to this encouragement with further efforts, building on their achievements, and so on. Using star and rewards charts with older children also works wonders when parents are trying to encourage positive behaviours. Positive reinforcement is a powerful tool that works with all age groups.

When supporting your child to overcome depression it can be helpful to consider the types of positive reinforcement strategies that will help you in this task. You may want to encourage your child to communicate more with the family or to engage in more activities, or to use CBT strategies for their depression, or to attend treatment appointments. None of these things are easy to do when a young person is feeling depressed. Finding ways to reward and reinforce these behaviours will help them to make the necessary positive steps towards recovery. If you decide to use rewards then keep in mind that this is not bribery. Using rewards to help someone make steps towards feeling better is a very useful and valid strategy.

What sort of reinforcement does your child respond to best?

- small rewards (e.g. magazine, sweet treat, phone credit, stationery, voucher)
- verbal praise (noticing when your child has done something well or has made an effort and letting them know you noticed this and that you are very pleased/proud/happy)
- saving money (e.g. working out a reward system that allows your child to receive and save money for something bigger that they would like to buy)
- time spent together doing things that your child wants to do (e.g. going out for a meal at their favourite restaurant, going to a fair/festival/show, going swimming or to the gym, playing their favourite game on Xbox)
- relaxing time together just doing nothing much or time together to discuss things and work through things
- subtle forms of praise from your body language or the

expression on your face (e.g. smiling and nodding when you notice them doing something positive for their depression)

- modelling how you treat and reward yourself when you have achieved something (e.g. 'I'm going to treat myself to a long bubble bath now because I completed that bit of work rather than putting it off')
- noticing and simply pointing out small achievements or small steps of progress towards goals ('It's great that you went to the gym this week')
- mentioning positive things you have noticed about your child to other people in the family, whether your child can hear this or not
- using a regular review time (see Chapter 13) with your child to note down the areas of progress
- surprising your child with a treat or day out and telling him/her how proud you are of them
- you know your child best so you may know what will feel rewarding for them
- or you may need to ask your child what they will find rewarding

Dealing with depression is not easy and giving your child appropriate positive reinforcement will provide additional encouragement on this journey. For example, if your child is trying to do some exercise as part of increasing their activity levels it might be a good idea to find ways to support this with rewards or acknowledgement and encouragement. Hopefully, your child will be rewarded for their efforts by an improvement in their mood but it will also be very rewarding for them to know that you are noticing their efforts. Supporting someone with depression is also very hard work and therefore we encourage you to notice and reward your own efforts on a regular basis.

Ideas for how to encourage and acknowledge my child's efforts:

Reward ideas

Things to say

My other responses

Things to do

Other ideas

My own treats for my efforts

12

Looking after yourself

Parent reflections:

'You really need to look after yourself. I know, it's easy to say. The thing is, looking after anyone with depression is hard work. There is no moment when the fever breaks, the temperature drops, the blood tests say "normal". There is only judgment. Considered judgment. Yours and the doctor's. This requires a degree of trust from a parent. You learn to trust the counselling, the professionals, your own judgment and your child. Like I said, at the end of this journey you will have grown. Growing is hard work and it takes energy! So look after yourself any way you can – swim, run, walk, get outside and away from your household environment for a while each day. Meet friends, eat well and give yourself and your depressed teenager some treats along the way.'

Research and clinical experience tells us that a young person with depression (and anxiety disorders) is much more likely to have a parent with depression and anxiety compared with young people who do not have these difficulties. As discussed earlier, there may be different reasons for this, such as genetic influences and a shared environment. Therefore, it's important to also pay attention to your own psychological health and any symptoms of depression or anxiety you or your partner may be experiencing. Some studies have shown that when a parent receives treatment for their depression and anxiety, their child's depression and anxiety improves as well, sometimes without even treating the child directly. It probably works the other way as well to some extent but this hasn't been studied enough. When both the parents and the child receive treatment this likely increases the chances of improvement for the child. Of course this makes a lot of sense. Parents who are dealing with their own difficulties are going to find it much harder also to deal with their child's low mood, and this may even add to their own depression and feelings of hopelessness.

As you may recall, one of the main things we witness when people are depressed is a tendency to see things in a hopeless and negative way. The other thing that often comes up for people who are depressed is a feeling that many things are their fault.

Can you imagine two people living with each other, both seeing things in an overly negative way and both blaming themselves unnecessarily for things that are not their fault?

This is a recipe for misunderstandings, arguments, over-reactions, avoidance-type behaviours, overly guilty feelings and low mood. It is possible that these interactions and feelings may actually fuel the depression for both family members.

Sue had been feeling quite low lately and she put it down to the stress of moving yet again and worrying about how everyone in the family was coping, especially Lin. On a few occasions Lin walked in on Sue crying in her bedroom and once in the kitchen. Sue quickly dried her eyes and told Lin not to worry, that she was just missing some of her friends and family but she was absolutely fine. Sue just couldn't snap out of it and noticed that she was finding it harder and harder to do the usual family things and to cope with work as well. She was also worrying more and more about Lin's mood and some days she just didn't have the energy to think about how she was going to help her daughter. She thought that once Lin settled in more and became happier, she too would feel much better.

Although Sue didn't know this, Lin also worried about her mother all the time. These worries were especially negative when Lin's mood was low. Both Lin and her mother were worrying about each other and this was impacting on both their moods.

Sue had gone to her GP and he suggested she was depressed and gave her a prescription for anti-depressants. Sue was initially determined to get better by herself but she was now more aware that she needed extra help. She decided to start taking the medication to see if it would make a difference. She also looked up a few counsellors in her area because she felt she needed to talk about her feelings with someone who was not in the family. Sue started to note down some of her thoughts when she was feeling low. She was surprised to find how often she had thoughts about failure: 'I'm a terrible mother and wife', 'I'm not good at anything', 'I'll never be successful', and about future difficulties: 'Nothing will get better', 'It's all so hopeless'. Sue began to work on these thoughts and look for evidence that didn't support this way of thinking.

Sue decided to tell Lin about how she had been feeling and what steps she was taking to help herself. Lin told her mum that she had already known for a while that she was really unhappy and this had worried her. Lin said she was glad that she was doing something about it. While Sue's decision to start medication and counselling didn't have any immediate effects on her low mood, it did help both Sue and Lin to feel more hopeful about things in general. Lin also felt relieved that her mum was getting some support. Lin started to think that perhaps she could look into ways of helping herself with her own mood and she mentioned this to her mother. Sue was really pleased to hear this and started to tell Lin about how she had been catching her negative thoughts and noting them down.

If you are struggling with depression, anxiety, or other mental health difficulties and are not already receiving treatment and support we urge you to do something about it. You may feel that by asking for treatment yourself you are somehow not being strong enough for the family. In fact, this may be the best thing that you can do for yourself and for your family. The better you feel, the more able you will be to support those who need you. On another level, you will be showing your child that it is OK to have these types of problems and it is fine to ask for help. This is a fantastic message to be sending out. Your child may have been worrying about you and if you show them that the right things are being put in place for you, this will reduce this worry and help your child to focus more on getting well too.

This highlights the importance of your modelling to your child every day. Even though teenagers are going through the process of becoming independent and separate from the family, it is important not to underestimate how much they still pay attention to their parents' behaviour for information and guidance. Often adolescents act as if their parents are hugely irritating or even irrelevant. They may be defiant, disagree with everything their parents say, stay away from home as much as possible, and avoid shared activities and outings, but teenagers are still picking up powerful and important messages from their parents all the time – it's just not terribly obvious that this is happening.

Therefore it is incredibly important to reflect on what you may be modelling from moment to moment. It's a great opportunity to help your teenager to take charge of their own low mood or other difficulties by showing them that you are able to take charge of your own problems. The messages you will be giving are that 'things can change', 'there are always ways to over-come difficulties' and 'it's OK to try things and to ask for help, if needed'. Another very important message to send out is that 'it's OK to reward and treat yourself for small achievements or simply for just being you'.

If you are experiencing low mood, as a start you might be able to apply some of the techniques in this book to your own diffi-culties, where appropriate. For example, have you withdrawn from activities that you previously enjoyed or is your life out of balance with too many stressful things and not enough calming and relaxing activities? If so, make a problem and goal list and and see if you can begin engaging in things that you know will help you feel better, even if it's just in a very small way. You can even share this with your child as a way of demonstrating some of the strategies that you would like them to apply. Have you also noticed that you experience a lot of negative thoughts? Perhaps you haven't had time to pay attention to this before. If you find there is a link between your low mood and negative thoughts then it will be useful for you to start making a record of these thoughts and situations. You can then work on chang-ing the way you think to help you change the way you feel. We have provided a worksheet for your own thought work on pages 304–10.

You may decide to seek the help of a trained therapist for your difficulties. Adult services for people with depression and anx-iety disorders are usually available via your GP on the NHS in most areas of the UK. The waiting times for treatment will vary so it is worth asking for a referral sooner rather than later. You can always cancel the appointment if you feel you no longer need it when it comes up. Of course there are also private therapists and counsellors if this is an option you can consider. It is important to check that the therapist is registered with the correct organizations so that you can be confident about their qualifications and quality of care. We have given a list of useful professional organizations at the back of this book. There is also a list of books for adults that you might find useful. The *Overcoming Depression* book is particularly helpful for adults who want to deal with their depressed mood and there are also online resources that are listed in the appendix.

Example: Sue's thought record

Situation – what's happening, who is there, where am I?

Lin comes home from school in tears, storms upstairs and slams her door.

My thoughts – what am I thinking about this situation? What am I predicting will happen? Do I have any memories, images about this?

'I can't handle this.'

'She's never going to get better.'

'She'll be held back in life and it will affect her in every way.'

'I'm obviously doing something wrong here.'

'I thought I was a good mother but how can I be when she's so upset all the time?'

'I'm failing at everything.'

Am I making any classic thinking errors? (e.g. predicting the worst, all or nothing thinking, fortune telling, etc.)

Predicting the worst.

Fortune telling, magnifying the worst.

Blaming myself for things that are not my fault.

All or nothing thinking.

My feelings – what am I feeling? Can I feel this in my body, what's that like?

Worried

Stressed

Low

Hopeless

Tense muscles

My responses – what do I do/not do to cope with these thoughts and feelings?

Less helpful responses
Avoid talking to Lin in case I can't cope and find out it's my fault.

Run straight upstairs to see what's happened.

Turn the situation over and over in my mind.

Cancel my plans with friends that evening.

Helpful responses

Write my thoughts and feelings down to get some distance and perspective.

Take a moment to gather my thoughts and feelings and to think about the best options before going upstairs to see Lin.

Stay calm and plan what to say to Lin.

Go out anyway after speaking with Lin.

What are the real facts of the situation (that is, not based on how I feel or what I may be thinking)?

The facts are that Lin has been getting better lately and she hasn't come home in this sort of mood for over two weeks now.

Just because she has bad days doesn't mean that she won't get better. I know people can get well and there is every chance that she will be fine in the future.

I know I am a good parent because I am trying my best and that's all that I can expect of myself.

My children are healthy and secure in many ways.

I have managed to help Lin already and I am also helping myself and getting help from others.

Taking the facts into account, is there a more balanced way in which I could think or see the situation?

There have been many positive signs lately that things are getting better. I just can't see them right now because I'm feeling low and worried.

I'm doing the best I can and there are many things that I am succeeding in.

With patience and perseverance we will continue to make progress.

There's always a way to find a solution and to be able to cope.

Does that make me feel differently? How do I feel now?

Less stressed and hopeless

A bit less low

Does it help me to respond in more helpful ways? How?

More confident about being able to deal with this situation in a helpful way.

Less inclined to either completely avoid dealing with it or to rush ahead without planning.

What do I do? What's the outcome?

Take a moment to go to the study to write down some thoughts.

Think about the best way to handle the situation. Decide to help Lin problem solve the difficulty, or if she is not responsive to this, just give her some support and tell her that I'm happy to talk when she's ready.

When I go upstairs a little later to talk to Lin I find out that she has had a bad day at school and has found out about a party she hasn't been invited to. I stay calm and listen. After a while I suggest that there might be things we can do about this to help her feel better. She doesn't want to do this but she agrees to stop looking at Facebook and to come downstairs and help me with dinner.

Later we look at the facts together and come up with a plan of how Lin will find out more about this party and why she hasn't been invited yet.

What have I learned that I might hold onto for the next time something like this comes up?

I can handle my daughter's distress if I stay calm and take some time out to think and plan!

How will I remember this for next time?

Tell myself 'STOP, THINK and PLAN' next time I feel stressed and overwhelmed. Remind myself that it's OK to feel this way and to take some time out to think.

My thought record

Situation – what's happening, where am I, who is there?

My thoughts – what am I thinking about in this situation? What am I predicting will happen? Do I have any memories, images about this?

Am I making any classic thinking errors? (e.g. predicting the worst, all or nothing thinking, fortune telling, etc.)

My feelings – How do I feel? What else am I feeling? Can I feel this in my body, what's that like?

My responses – what do I do/not do to cope with these thoughts and feelings?

Less helpful responses

Helpful responses

What are the real facts of the situation (that is, not based on how I feel or what I may be thinking)?

Taking the facts into account, is there a more balanced way I could think or see the situation?

Does that make me feel differently? How do I feel now?

Does it help me to respond in more helpful ways? How?

What do I do? What's the outcome?

What have I learned that I might hold onto for the next time something like this comes up?

How will I remember this for next time?

Part 5

Keeping progress going

13

Planning for the future and getting more help

As with any worthwhile endeavour, overcoming depression involves ups and downs and it is seldom a straightforward journey. It is inevitable that at times things will seem to improve, at other times it will feel as though nothing is changing at all, and sometimes things will seem to feel worse for a while. This is perfectly normal and in fact it is to be expected. Anyone who has recovered from depression may be able to describe their journey in this way and it is not common to hear that recovery was a simple straight line from A to B.

Planning for these different phases can be very helpful because it will prepare you and your child for what to do in these times. Often it is the more difficult times that are the most valuable because they provide an opportunity for you and your child to learn how to cope and to practise the strategies that are most helpful for their situation. When things are going well it is harder to remember to practise the strategies and they sometimes get completely forgotten about. So we encourage you to view the slower and tougher times as good opportunities to learn and practise. We can't stress enough how important it is to carry on using the strategies and to give each method a fair run before deciding whether it is helpful or not. This might mean consistent practise of each strategy for at least a few weeks.

It is easy to get disheartened when things seem to be going much slower than you want. For example, your child may start to do some of the things that they previously enjoyed but you notice that it is far from what things used to be like and there are still lots of bad days.

At this point both you and your child have a choice about how to respond to this. You can either become frustrated, angry or hopeless because you have thoughts such as 'it's just not working', 'it will never get better', 'why is it taking so long?', 'what's the point?' and so on.

The other option is to notice every single change and to collect all the evidence, no matter how small, that things are moving forward in the right direction. It is about noticing all the very small things and small changes and then putting them all together. It's as if you were collecting dewdrops into a cup from leaves in your garden. Initially you will have only a few drops at the bottom of the cup and you will hardly be able to see it. At this point you may become discouraged and shake the liquid out and give up altogether, which will get you back to square one. But if you keep going, before you know it, you will have collected half a cup and the liquid will be much more visible. In other words, we encourage you to develop thoughts such as 'we are taking it one step at a time', 'it's moving in the right direction', 'there is some progress already', 'it might take a bit of time and patience', 'this is an opportunity to learn many valuable things' and so on.

As you become familiar with the methods in this book you will undoubtedly notice that some things seem relevant and helpful to you and your child while others don't fit at all. You may have also noticed and picked up strategies and ideas that are not in this book at all but seem to work for your child and your family. Perhaps you have been able to talk with others or to discuss ideas with your child's therapist if they are receiving treatment. Regardless of where the helpful strategies have come from, it's really useful to summarize the things that seem to work for your individual situation.

In this chapter we encourage you to **note down any strategies that have been helpful to you and/or your child** and **plan how to keep using these**. There are also tips about how to **spot the warning signs early on** to reduce the chance of depression coming back or getting worse in the future.

Things that have helped

Having a better understanding of depression ☐

Understanding symptoms of depression and the impact of ☐
these on my child

Understanding the background to how the depression ☐
started

Understanding what may be keeping my child's depression ☐
going

Setting achievable goals ☐

Hearing about other parents' experiences ☐

Knowing that depression is common and that others are in ☐
similar situations

Putting together an emergency plan for risky behaviour ☐

Knowing where to seek further help and support ☐

Talking to the GP and getting GP involved in my child's care ☐

Getting referred to other services ☐

Talking to other parents/teachers/others ☐

Understanding the importance of food, exercise and sleep ☐

Having ideas about how to tackle sleeping issues ☐

Getting more information and facts about depression ☐

Understanding the CBT links and how CBT works ☐

Understanding how activity helps ☐

Encouraging my child to be more active and to do things ☐
they used to enjoy

Regularly reviewing goals and thinking about my child's life ☐
values

Understanding the close link between thoughts and feelings ☐

Helping my child to change the way they are thinking ☐

Setting up fact finders and putting things to the test ☐

Helping my child with solving problems ☐

Considering the role of stress in depression ☐

Considering any communication problems and improving
family communication ☐

Keeping expectations realistic ☐

Using positive reinforcement more often ☐

Looking after my own needs and mental health ☐

Looking up websites or contacting other organizations for ☐
more information and help

Other advice and strategies that seem to work for my child
and my family:

_____

_____

_____

_____

_____

_____

_____

Things that are better, the same, worse

If you used the **Short Mood and Feelings Questionnaire** (see pages 11–12) with your child, what is the score now?

Total score now _____ Date _____

How does that compare with earlier scores?

Think back to the original goals for your child (see pages 53–6). How much progress has been made in relation to those goals? Are there new goals that could be set?

Goal 1 _____ Progress   0 1 2 3 4 5 6 7 8 9 10
(0 = no progress at all, 10 = I've totally reached my goal)

Goal 2 _____ Progress   0 1 2 3 4 5 6 7 8 9 10
(0 = no progress at all, 10 = I've totally reached my goal)

Goal 3 _____ Progress   0 1 2 3 4 5 6 7 8 9 10
(0 = no progress at all, 10 = I've totally reached my goal)

Things/symptoms that seem to be better:

_____

_____

_____

_____

_____

Things/symptoms that have stayed the same:

_____

_____

_____

_____

_____

Things/symptoms that have got worse:

_____

_____

_____

_____

_____

New goals

1. _____

2. _____

3. _____

4. _____

Ways to remember to apply the strategies

As mentioned above, it's important to keep practising and using the strategies in order to see faster progress. You may need to remind your child regularly to apply the things that have been helpful to them. It's a good idea to also practise things when your child is having a relatively OK day or few days so that it becomes easier for them to remember what to do in times of greater stress or on worse days. If you can encourage your child to see these strategies as habits then it will become automatic and it will feel much less of an effort. For example, you may have encouraged your child to evaluate his or her thoughts and to try to think differently. To help make this strategy become more of a habit, when you notice your child engaging in negative thinking you may be able to simply say a reminder phrase, such as 'is it the negative thinking again?', which may be enough to help them make a change there and then.

It might make sense to have a list of useful strategies some-where to hand, such as on the wall of your child's bedroom or even on the fridge. It doesn't have to be a long list or to be overly serious. It could be called something like the following:

Proven stress reducers or helpful ideas for my mood

What am I feeling right now? Name it.

What can I do about it?

Go for a walk/jog

Have I eaten enough?

Are my thoughts telling me how it is rather than looking at the evidence?

What can I do right now that will relax me?

Do I need to solve a problem?

Do I need more help from someone?

Ideally, if you can set aside half an hour each week to review progress this will help you to keep on the right track. This might be a regular slot each week that you know tends to be a quiet time for your family. During this time you could reflect on your own or think together with your child about progress on the goals and about which strategies seem to be helping and how to use these more often.

Chosen day and time for reviewing progress:

Triggers and warning signs that depression may be coming back

With time, the right treatment and regular effort your child's depression will get better. Once the depression improves it will be helpful to keep in mind a list of warning signs that may indicate his or her depression could be resurfacing. It has been found that some (although not all) young people who experience depression will go on to have another episode of depression later on. Catching the early warning signs and being aware of the triggers means a better chance of reducing the likelihood of this happening.

For some people the trigger event may be going through particularly stressful times, or it could be situations that involve falling out with friends. For others the early warning sign may be a gradual withdrawal from activities. Opposite is an example list of triggers and early warning signs to be aware of and to look out for, and a space for you to add any others that are particularly relevant for your child.

Has my child stopped usual activities? ❏

Is my child spending a lot of time on their own, do they seem withdrawn? ❏

Is my child having any relationship difficulties? ❏

Is my child facing additional stresses? ❏

Is my child eating less or more than usual, or a lot of junk food? ❏

Do they seem more sensitive, emotional or tearful? ❏

Is there obvious avoidance of things/people? ❏

Have I noticed a change in their sleeping pattern or do they seem to be extra tired/yawning a lot? ❏

Is my child cancelling appointments or making excuses not to do things? ❏

Has my child stopped any hobbies or is not enjoying usual activities? ❏

Do they seem more irritable than usual? ❏

Has my child stopped relaxing activities (is there a good balance)? ❏

Does my child seem very unmotivated or does everything seem like a big effort? ❏

Is my child spending too much time in bed? ❏

Do they seem to be over-reacting or very stressed about little things? ❏

Is my child feeling more anxious about things? ❏

Is my child having concentration difficulties? ❏

Are they arguing more with me or the family? ❏

Are there stressful events or big changes coming up soon
(e.g. new school/uni)

☐

Is my child taking less care of their appearance?

☐

Other possible warning signs:

_____

_____

_____

_____

_____

_____

_____

_____

_____

Our plan for when we notice the warning signs

Strategies to use:

Things that may need to change:

Problems that may need to be solved:

People/organizations who will need to help:

The best order for our plan:

First step:

Second step:

Third step:

Other notes and ideas:

Some final thoughts from a parent

The following thoughts have been very generously shared by a parent who has gone through this journey with their child, and positively come out the other side. We hope that it helps you towards your own journey.

Happy Ending

'When you choose to undertake and then have taken this journey with your child you have become extremely close. Even though you keep your distance, have your own friends, jobs, hobbies and interests, you have forged a bond that is supremely strong.

'You have done the equivalent of climbing Everest together! Those experiences will stay with you both.

'However, as a parent, you need to remember that they will grow up and no longer need you to such an obvious extent. This is what you have been trying to achieve after all! An independent adult is your goal. Of course this is the goal of all parenting and we are very happy when we get there. But you need to know that if you have been a strong facilitator of your child's healing and growth it is going to hurt like hell, even when they get better!

'So you've done the journey as far as CAMHS (Child and Adolescent Mental Health Services) takes you ... your job now is to quietly, confidently, let your young adult take charge. You need to step back. Having been maybe the instigator of the particular route of the journey up to now, the route from now on is of your child's making.

'When such an emotional period has come to an end, the baton, the toolbox of life, if you like, having now been handed to the child, there is yet another hurdle for the parent ... you grieve. You don't grieve because they are well, you don't grieve because they have grown up, you grieve for all that you have been through together. At last you have the perspective to see where you have been. When you are at the summit, shrouded in mist, you cannot see. Once safely at base camp you look back at where you have been and you realize what you have accomplished together. BUT, it remains your job to now quietly confidently move on, just like your child. It is important that this period of growth is now integrated. For both of you. You do not now need to be the parent of a depressed teenager!

'Let it go and smile!

'**Good luck, and we wish your child, you and your family all the very best.**'

Appendix 1

Summary of useful places to find more info and help

Information about depression and CBT

National Institute of Clinical Excellence (NICE) – information about depression in young people and evidence-based treatment.

www.nice.org.uk/CG28

Young Minds – information, advice, support and helplines for young people affected by mental health problems, and their parents.

www.youngminds.org.uk

Parents' helpline: 0808 802 5544
(Monday–Friday, 9.30 a.m.–4 p.m.)

www.youngminds.org.uk/for_parents

Royal College of Psychiatrists – information for young people and parents about mental health and a range of related topics. www.rcpsych.ac.uk/healthadvice/parentsandyouthinfo.aspx

www.rcpsych.ac.uk/expertadvice.aspx

www.rcpsych.ac.uk/mentalhealthinformation/therapies/cognitivebehaviouraltherapy.aspx

British Association for Behavioural and Cognitive Psychotherapies (BABCP) – organization providing information about CBT and accreditation of CBT therapists. Register of practising therapists in your area.

www.babcp.com/public/what-is-cbt.aspx

NHS Choices

Information from the National Health Service on conditions, treatments, local services and healthy living.

www.nhs.uk/conditions/cognitive-behavioural-therapy/pages/Introduction.aspx

Further information, support and advice

Depression Alliance – national charity providing information and articles about depression.

www.depressionalliance.org

Family Lives – dedicated organization supporting parents and different aspects of family life. Support, advice and help available from trained family support workers. Support available online and on email, live chat and telephone.

Helpline: 0808 800 2222

www.familylives.org.uk

Charlie Waller Memorial Trust – Charity organization committed to raising awareness about depression and mental health problems in young people and reducing the stigma. Offers useful information and further contacts, and brief parent guide.

www.cwmt.org.uk

Rethink – information and helpline for anyone affected by mental health problems.

Helpline: 0300 500 0927 (Monday–Friday, 10 a.m.–2 p.m.)

www.rethink.org

Mental Health Foundation – information about mental health and related issues.

www.mentalhealth.org.uk

Mind – information on mental health problems and treatments.

Helpline: 0300 123 3393 (Monday–Friday, 9 a.m.–6 p.m.)

www.mind.org.uk

Cruse – support and helpline for bereaved people and those caring for bereaved people.

Helpline: 0844 477 9400 (Monday–Friday, 9.30 a.m.–5 p.m. and until 8 p.m. Tuesday–Thursday)

www.cruse.org.uk

Crisis support and information

ChildLine – free confidential 24-hour helpline or online chat service for **young people** up to nineteen years of age.

Helpline: 0800 1111 (24 hours)

www.childline.org.uk

Samaritans – free confidential 24-hour helpline for anyone needing support.

Helpline: 08457 909090 (24 hours)

www.samaritans.org

Papyrus HOPELineUK – free confidential helpline or online support for anyone having suicidal thoughts, or for anyone concerned about a young person at risk of harming themselves.

Helpline: 0800 068 4141 (Monday–Friday, 10 a.m.–10 p.m.; Saturday–Sunday, 2 p.m.–5 p.m.)

www.papyrus-uk.org/support/for-you

www.papyrus-uk.org/support/for-parents

Harmless – support for people who self-harm, and support for the families and friends of those who self-harm.

www.harmless.org.uk

Social Services – support for young people and families affected by a range of difficulties or for anyone concerned about the welfare of a young person. Find your local service via your council website or in the local directory.

NSPCC – information and helplines for anyone concerned about a young person.

Helpline: 0808 800 5000 (24 hours)

www.nspcc.org.uk

Adfam – support and advice for families affected by drugs and alcohol.

www.adfam.org.uk

FRANK – confidential information and advice about drugs, offering online chat as well as a texting service.

Helpline: 0300 123 6600 (24 hours)

www.talktofrank.com

Drinkline – confidential information, help and advice for anyone affected by alcohol.

Helpline: 0300 123 1110 (Monday–Friday, 9 a.m.–8 p.m.; Saturday–Sunday, 11 a.m.–4 p.m.)

www.patient.co.uk/support/drinkline

Alcohol Concern – information about the harmful effects of alcohol.

www.alcoholconcern.org.uk

Bullying UK – advice and support for anyone affected by bullying.

Helpline: 0808 800 2222 (every day, 7 a.m.–midnight; calls diverted to the Samaritans at other times)

www.bullying.co.uk

Further self-help resources

NHS – self-help and information about exercise for depression.

www.nhs.uk/Conditions/stress-anxiety-depression/Pages/
exercise-for-depression.aspx

Moodgym – web-based CBT programme.

www.moodgym.anu.edu.au

Students Against Depression – information, support and
self-help ideas.

http://studentsagainstdepression.org

http://studentsagainstdepression.org/
understand-depression/why-me-why-now

Moodjuice – self-help booklet for people experiencing
depression.

www.moodjuice.scot.nhs.uk/depression.asp

Living Life to the Full – range of booklets, worksheets and
computer-based self-help modules.

www.livinglifetothefull.com or www.llttf.com

GET Self Help – free worksheets and CBT tools.

www.getselfhelp.co.uk/freedownloads2.htm

Information about healthy eating

http://studentsagainstdepression.org/tackle-depression/
healthier-daily-routine/understanding-food-and-mood/

http://mindfulcharity.ca/pdf/Teen_Resources_101.pdf

http://www.nhs.uk/Livewell/Goodfood/Pages/eatwell-plate.
aspx

Mindfulness and compassion

Be Mindful – information about how mindfulness can reduce
depression, anxiety and stress.

www.bemindful.co.uk

Mindful Youth – information about mindfulness young people

http://mindfulyouth.org

The Compassionate Mind Foundation – promoting wellbeing
through compassion.

www.compassionatemind.co.uk

Books

C. Creswell & L. Willetts, *Overcoming Your Child's Fears and Worries: A Self-Help Guide Using Cognitive Behavioral Techniques* (London: Constable & Robinson, 2007) – aimed at children up to twelve–thirteen years old but packed full of helpful strategies that can be adapted for older children with anxiety.

N. Dummett & C. Williams, *Overcoming Teenage Low Mood and Depression: A Five Areas Approach* (London: Hodder Arnold, 2008).

P. Gilbert, *Overcoming Depression: A Self-Help Guide Using Cognitive Behavioral Techniques* (London: Constable & Robinson, 2009).

K. Mears & M. Freeston, *Overcoming Worry: A Self-Help Guide Using Cognitive Behavioral Techniques* (London: Constable & Robinson, 2008).

L. Seiler, *Cool Connections with Cognitive Behavioural Therapy: Encouraging Self-Esteem, Resilience and Well-Being in Children and Young People Using CBT Approaches* (London: Jessica Kingsley Publishers, 2008).

Appendix 2

How to find a therapist

There are a few different ways to get a bit of extra help with some of the ideas in this book. There are places you can get help by telephone, text or email, and we have suggested several of these in Appendix 1.

You might prefer to get some extra help for your child from a professional therapist.

There are many different kinds of therapy. Only some forms of therapy are recommended for depression in young people. These are CBT (which is what this book is based on), family therapy, interpersonal therapy and psychodynamic psychotherapy. The therapist should be able to explain what each form of therapy is about and how it can help.

What should I expect if my child sees a therapist?

Most people don't know what goes on in therapy; after all, therapy usually happens behind closed doors. We think it's important to know what to expect. This can help your child get the best out of therapy. Here are some questions that many people ask and worry about.

Feel free to show this section to your child so that they can get some answers.

What do I have to talk about?

Seeing a therapist, especially at the start, can be very nerve-wracking. Don't worry if you can't think what to say or don't know where to start. Your therapist will be used to people being nervous and they will do everything possible to help you feel more at ease. If it is helpful you can ask a parent, carer or friend to come with you to therapy sessions. If you do not want this to happen you should tell your therapist and usually this is absolutely fine.

Will the therapist keep things private?

Your therapist will talk to you about confidentiality. Normally everything you tell them will be kept private but there may be times when this is not possible. Your therapist will explain when they would not be able to keep your discussions private.

Why does my therapist want to record our sessions?

Some CBT therapists will record your therapy sessions on video or audio. They use the recordings in supervision. Supervision is where their work is checked. This means that they are able to work effectively and safely. Your therapist will explain this to you and ask for permission to record the session. You don't have to agree but it is very helpful if you do. It helps make sure that you and everybody else gets the best possible help.

How will my therapist treat me?

When you start therapy you start a new relationship with a person you didn't know before. Your therapist should listen to you, accept you as a person, be warm and empathic, and understand your point of view. The bond or relationship you develop with your therapist is a very important part of having CBT or any other therapy. Trust is an important part of your relationship. Your therapist should be open with you at all times. They should tell you what therapy will involve, how long it will take, and how it will work.

It's important to feel respected by your therapist and to feel 'heard'. Your therapist is going to be older than you and will have had quite a lot of training and experience. They have expertise in being a therapist. This can make it hard for you to feel like you can be real partners but you have more experience than they do about your life, about what it is like to be you, and about what you want in the future. So you each bring your own expertise and this is the partnership. You will have lots of ways to take part and even to lead the therapy.

What will I have to do?

Therapy is about working together. That's right – you and your therapist are partners. CBT, in particular, is about

collaboration. This means that you decide together what you are going to try to change, you agree how to try to change, and you both take responsibility for what you do.

You know what **you** want to be different. Your CBT therapist will help you identify these goals in your first few sessions. It's important that you are able to play a full part in therapy. At the beginning of each session you and your therapist will agree on the agenda for this session. This means that you decide what you will do during the session and what is most important.

We've used the word 'work' to describe what happens in therapy. This is because therapy is not something that is done to you. It is something you take part in and put effort into. That's how real change happens – there really aren't any shortcuts.

What's this about homework?

In CBT, you and your therapist will develop *assignments* for you to do between sessions. We think assignments are a better word to use than 'homework'. This is because you and your therapist set assignments together. These are important because they help you change in the real world, outside of therapy. Therapy only lasts for an hour a week and will come to an end. Assignments help you to bridge the space between therapy sessions. They will also help you to learn and practise new skills and new ways of behaving and thinking.

A lot of CBT assignments will look like the exercises in this book. If you don't want to do an assignment or feel it is wrong, tell your therapist – don't forget you are partners and collaborators. You can help decide on something else that suits you better.

What if my therapist asks me to do something I don't want to?

Sometimes when you have therapy you discover that you have to face your fears in order to overcome them. This can be very, very difficult and frightening. Your therapist should be able to explain why it is important and it's important that you understand this. But it will not make it any easier. The trust you have in your therapist and the strength of your relationship will help you face your fears. You will not be asked to do anything against your will but you may decide that you do have to do things you find very difficult. Your therapist will help you to find and use different kinds of support.

How long will therapy last?

There are different stages of therapy. In CBT your therapist will explain how long therapy is likely to last (how many sessions over how many weeks). You will review this from time to time to see if it needs to change. The number of therapy sessions you have is hard to predict. It's unlikely that you would have more than twenty sessions. Each session will last about an hour.

During the first few sessions you and your therapist get to know each other and build trust and confidence. Your therapist will want to find out about you – about important things in your life and in your past, and about your strengths and weaknesses, and your hopes and dreams. You will identify your goals – what it is that you want to change. Your therapist is likely to ask you to fill in some questionnaires. These give them more information about your difficulties. Together you will build an understanding of your problems. This is called a **formulation**. The formulation is like a story of your life so far. It will include things that might have caused your problems or made them worse, and things that keep them going.

In the middle part of therapy you will work together to tackle your difficulties. You will focus on changing the things that keep your problems going. Most likely these will be your behaviours (like avoiding things) or your thoughts. You will try out different ways to think and to behave. You will have assignments between sessions and will build on these at each session. You and your therapist will monitor how you are doing and change your plans depending on how things go. You may go a bit faster, or a bit slower than expected. You might add some goals and take away other ones.

Therapy will end. The final stage of therapy prepares you to move on and live the rest of your life. It's important to see therapy as a stepping stone to prepare you for your best possible future.

Where can I find a therapist for my child?

Usually the best place to start is with your GP. If you live in the UK he or she can refer your child to specialist mental health services for young people. Some specialist services let you refer yourself without going to your GP but this is different in different parts of the county. If you search the Internet for 'Child and Adolescent Mental Health Services' in your nearest town or city you will find where they are and if they take direct referrals.

There might also be counselling services at your child's school or college that your child can use without going to the GP.

Finally, some therapists work privately. This means that you have to pay them for their help. Your GP is probably the best person to talk to about this but you can also find private therapists by contacting specific organizations (e.g. BABCP, British Psychological Society, your insurance company if you have health insurance).

What do I need to know about my child's therapist?

Finding a therapist is not very difficult but there are a few things to keep in mind to make sure your child gets the right help.

There are a lot of different kinds of people who offer therapy.

Psychotherapists, therapists and counsellors

Anyone can call themselves a 'therapist' or a 'psychotherapist' or a 'counsellor', even after a two-day training course. So it's important to ask them questions about their training. A good therapist will be pleased that you asked them and will give you as much information as you want.

The information in this book is based on a form of psychological therapy known as CBT – cognitive behaviour therapy. In the UK and many other countries face-to-face CBT is recommended for young people who have depression. If your son or daughter has mild depression, self-help CBT, like we use in this book, is recommended.

If you want to work with a therapist using the same ideas as we have talked about in this book you should ask to be referred for CBT. Your therapist should have had special training in CBT and should also have regular supervision to make sure that their work is as good as it can be.

Some CBT therapists are nurses, occupational therapists, social workers or some other kind of professional. They will have done an extra one-year course to train in CBT. After this, if they have the right kind of experience and supervision, they can register as a CBT therapist with the British Association of Behavioural and Cognitive Psychotherapy (BABCP). If they are registered (accredited) with the BABCP you can look them up on the BABCP website – www.babcp.org.

If your therapist is accredited by the BABCP they have to have regular supervision, keep up to date with the research, and have regular updates to their training. Their registration is renewed every five years. If they do anything wrong they can be 'struck off' the register. If you are offered CBT by a therapist who is not a psychologist you should make sure that they are accredited by the BABCP.

Clinical and counselling psychologists

In the UK no one is allowed to call himself or herself a 'clinical psychologist' or a 'counselling psychologist' unless they are registered and listed on the Health and Care Professions Council (HCPC). These titles are protected by law. You can check that they are registered by going to the HCPC website and searching for their name – www.hcpc-uk.org. Anyone at all can say they are a 'psychologist'. Be aware, they do not have to be registered and may not have the right training.

All registered clinical and counselling psychologists have completed an undergraduate degree in psychology and post-graduate training, which is usually for three years. This is usually a doctorate degree so most clinical and counselling psychologists will have the title 'Doctor'. Psychologists are regulated by the HCPC and they have to stick to rules and regulations about the best and safest ways to practice.

Psychologists often specialize in different types of therapy, including CBT. But not all psychologists offer CBT or have special training, so it is important to ask them. They may offer family therapy or interpersonal therapy for depression and these are also recommended for young people. The best way to find out if they offer CBT is to ask them. Some psychologists are also accredited with the BABCP but it is not required for them to practice CBT.

Other professionals

If your child is referred to the NHS for help with depression you might meet other kinds of professionals. For example, if they are prescribed anti-depressant medication this will be by a psychiatrist. A psychiatrist is a medical doctor who specializes in mental health. They will see your child again to review or alter the medication, if necessary.

Your child might also be seen by a nurse or a primary care mental health worker. They may be able to support your child using CBT techniques but they cannot offer CBT unless they have had specialist training and supervision. They may be trained in other effective therapies such as family therapy or interpersonal therapy. Feel free to ask, all good therapists are happy to discuss their training and experience.

Appendix 3

Copies of worksheets

My child's mood summary

Symptoms observed

Symptoms reported by my child

How long have symptoms been around for (more than two weeks)?

How often are the symptoms coming up (almost every day)?

Any obvious things that make it worse

Ways in which symptoms are interfering (at school, with friends, at home)

Any concerning behaviours or thoughts (e.g. risky behaviours or suicidal thoughts)

Things that seem to help

My child's problem list

My child's agreed goals

Long-term goals

Medium-term goals

Short-term goals

Copies of worksheets

Progress chart

Weeks 1/2

Goal 1 _____ Progress   0 1 2 3 4 5 6 7 8 9 10
(0 = no progress at all, 10 = completely reached my goal)

Goal 2 _____ Progress   0 1 2 3 4 5 6 7 8 9 10
(0 = no progress at all, 10 = completely reached my goal)

Goal 3 _____ Progress   0 1 2 3 4 5 6 7 8 9 10
(0 = no progress at all, 10 = completely reached my goal)

Weeks 3/4

Goal 1 _____ Progress   0 1 2 3 4 5 6 7 8 9 10
(0 = no progress at all, 10 = completely reached my goal)

Goal 2 _____ Progress   0 1 2 3 4 5 6 7 8 9 10
(0 = no progress at all, 10 = completely reached my goal)

Goal 3 _____ Progress   0 1 2 3 4 5 6 7 8 9 10
(0 = no progress at all, 10 = completely reached my goal)

355

Weeks 5/6

Goal 1 _____ Progress   0 1 2 3 4 5 6 7 8 9 10
(0 = no progress at all, 10 = completely reached my goal)

Goal 2 _____ Progress   0 1 2 3 4 5 6 7 8 9 10
(0 = no progress at all, 10 = completely reached my goal)

Goal 3 _____ Progress   0 1 2 3 4 5 6 7 8 9 10
(0 = no progress at all, 10 = completely reached my goal)

Weeks 7/8

Goal 1 _____ Progress   0 1 2 3 4 5 6 7 8 9 10
(0 = no progress at all, 10 = completely reached my goal)

Goal 2 _____ Progress   0 1 2 3 4 5 6 7 8 9 10
(0 = no progress at all, 10 = completely reached my goal)

Goal 3 _____ Progress   0 1 2 3 4 5 6 7 8 9 10
(0 = no progress at all, 10 = completely reached my goal)

Weeks 9/10

Goal 1 _____ Progress   0 1 2 3 4 5 6 7 8 9 10
(0 = no progress at all, 10 = completely reached my goal)

Goal 2 _____ Progress   0 1 2 3 4 5 6 7 8 9 10
(0 = no progress at all, 10 = completely reached my goal)

Goal 3 _____ Progress   0 1 2 3 4 5 6 7 8 9 10
(0 = no progress at all, 10 = completely reached my goal)

Weeks 11/12

Goal 1 _____ Progress   0 1 2 3 4 5 6 7 8 9 10
(0 = no progress at all, 10 = completely reached my goal)

Goal 2 _____ Progress   0 1 2 3 4 5 6 7 8 9 10
(0 = no progress at all, 10 = completely reached my goal)

Goal 3 _____ Progress   0 1 2 3 4 5 6 7 8 9 10
(0 = no progress at all, 10 = completely reached my goal)

My emergency toolkit

People your child will contact when having suicidal thoughts/urges to self-harm,

for example:

1. Mother and/or father: face to face or mobile numbers 00000 000000 and 00000 000000

2. Other relative, e.g. brother: mobile 00000 000000, landline 00000 000000

3. School nurse/teacher: face to face

4. GP: GP telephone number and out of hours number

5. Responsible friend: mobile 00000 000000

6. Support organizations or crisis phone numbers (e.g. ChildLine or Samaritans, see Appendix 1, note the telephone numbers down)

7. Nearest A&E department for on-call psychiatrist

Triggers that seem to make your child's mood worse or increase the likelihood of suicidal thoughts and/or urges to self-harm, for example:

1. Arguments with friends/family

2. Spending too much time on social media sites

3.   Spending too much time alone

4.   Substances (e.g. alcohol)

5.   Bullying or being in trouble with the law

List of useful distractions, for example:

1.   Watching a funny programme on television

2.   Helping with gardening or dinner

3.   Going for a jog/walk/to the gym/drawing

4.   Phoning someone

List of other coping strategies to prevent harm, for example:

1.   Writing feelings down

2.   Punching a pillow or screaming into the pillow

3.   Listening to uplifting music

4.   Flicking a rubber band against the skin, putting an ice cube on the skin or pinching (instead of cutting)

My sleep diary

Complete the diary every day. It's probably best to do it first thing in the morning

	Day 1	Day 2	Day 3	Day 4	Day 5	Day 6	Day 7
What time did you go to bed?							
How long did it take you to go to sleep?							
How many times did you wake up in the night?							
After falling asleep how long were you awake for during the night?							
At what time did you wake up (the last time)?							
What time did you get up and out of bed?							
How long in total did you spend in bed?							
How well did you sleep? (1 = very bad, 5 = very good)							

My child's cycles

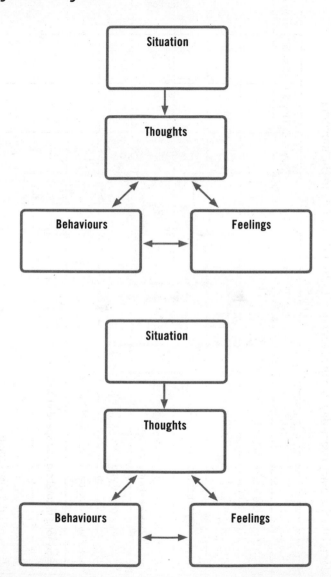

Teenage Depression

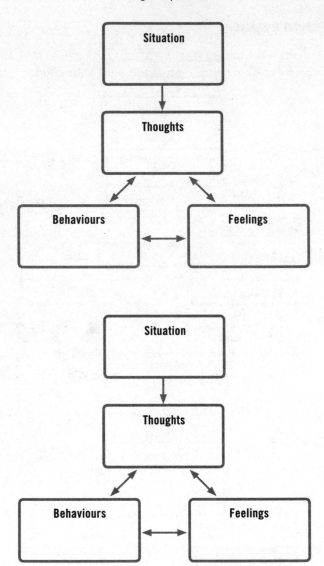

My own cycles

You might want to take the opportunity to have a think about your own cycles in specific situations with your child:

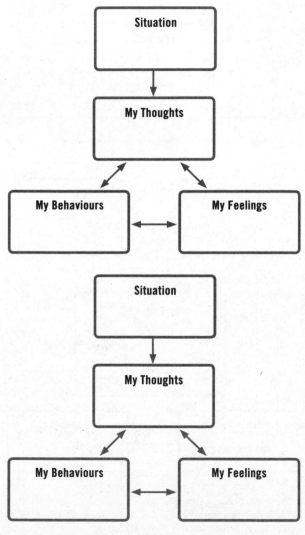

Our cycles together

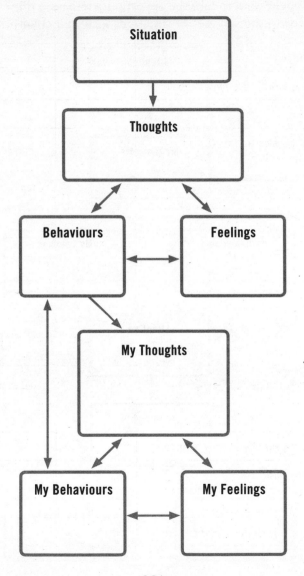

Activity list

Physical activity	Do now?	Used to do?
Swimming		
Playing sport (e.g. tennis, football)		
Dancing		
Other physical activity (e.g. riding, running, cycling)		
Skills/work/education	**Do now?**	**Used to do?**
Learning to drive		
Paid work (e.g. babysitting, paper round)		
School		
Homework		
Music lesson		
Creative things	**Do now?**	**Used to do?**
Drama		
Art (e.g. painting, drawing, sculpture)		
Playing music		
Cooking		
Writing (e.g. stories, diary, poetry)		

Being sociable/relationships	Do now?	Used to do?
Watching TV with family		
Having a family meal		
Shopping with friends		
Voluntary work		
Spending time with family and friends		
Having fun	**Do now?**	**Used to do?**
Going to the cinema		
Playing computer games		
Going to a party		
Having friends to stay overnight		
Planning a party or social event		

My activity log – today's date _____

Copies of worksheets

Date, time	Activity – what I did, with whom and where	Achievement	Closeness	Enjoyment	Important?
7 a.m.–8 a.m.					
8 a.m.–9 a.m.					
9 a.m.–10 a.m.					
10 a.m.–11 a.m.					
11 a.m.–12 noon					
12 noon–1 p.m.					
1 p.m.–2 p.m.					
2 p.m.–3 p.m.					
3 p.m.–4 p.m.					
4 p.m.–5 p.m.					
5 p.m.–6 p.m.					

Teenage Depression

	6 p.m.–7 p.m.	7 p.m.–8 p.m.	8 p.m.–9 p.m.	9 p.m.–10 p.m.	10 p.m.–11 p.m.	11 p.m.–12 midnight	12 midnight–1 a.m.	1 a.m.–2 a.m.	2 a.m.–3 a.m.	3 a.m.–4 a.m.	4 a.m.–5 a.m.	5 a.m.–6 a.m.	6 a.m.–7 a.m	7 a.m.–8 a.m.

368

My life values

What is important to you about each of these areas?

Me	Things that matter	People that matter
Hobbies/fun	Education and work	Family
Keeping healthy	Things I need to do	Friends
Looking after myself	The bigger picture	Boyfriend/girlfriend

My thought-catching log

Time and date	Situation – what happened	What you thought\n\nHow much you believe it	Feeling\n\nHow strong is the feeling?

Copies of worksheets

Thinking Traps

Black and white thinking (or all or nothing thinking)

'I *must* make a good impression at this party or I'll *never* make friends.'

'If I don't get an A in the exam it'll prove how stupid I am.'

....

(Your example)

Over-generalizing

'She's cross with me; I know that she hates me, everyone hates me.'

'If she doesn't invite me to her party I'll *never* make any new friends.'

....

(Your example)

Predicting the worst

'I'm bound to fail that exam. My life will be ruined. I'll never get to college, or get a good job.'

'I'll hate that party; no one will speak to me.'

'She'll stop being my friend.'

....

(Your example)

Self-blaming

'It's because I'm stupid/ugly/horrible/unlovable.'

'I've let everyone down.'

....

(Your example)

Mind reading

'She'll think I'm stupid.'

'They all think I'm ugly.'

'My parents will be so disappointed in me.'

....

(Your example)

Jumping to conclusions

'If I don't get picked for the team I'll be so embarrassed, I won't be able to play again.'

'Where are they? They're late. They're not coming. I've been stood up.'

'They're whispering. I bet they're talking about me.'

....

(Your example)

My child's more helpful thoughts

Situation _____

Thought	Feeling How strong? 0–100 per cent	New, more helpful thought	Feeling How strong? 0–100 per cent

My Child's fact finder

Thought(s) to test
Fact finder
Prediction
Do it

So what happened?

Was the prediction right?

What does it all mean?

Is there a balanced view?

What's next?

My child's problem solving

STEP 1 Name it:

The problem is

_____

_____

_____

_____

_____

STEP 2 Come up with some possible solutions – go on, add some funny and ridiculous ones too, it helps with imagination.

_____

_____

_____

_____

_____

_____

_____

STEP 3 Have a think about each solution and how good you think it is – will it solve the problem completely or maybe even just a little?

_____

_____

_____

_____

_____

_____

STEP 4 Choose one or two of your favourite solutions – they don't have to be perfect, in fact most of the time solutions are not perfect, they're just OK.

My favourite solutions are

_____

_____

_____

_____

_____

_____

STEP 5 Plan how and when you will try them out.

_____

_____

_____

_____

_____

_____

_____

STEP 6 Try them. Did it work?

_____

_____

_____

_____

_____

_____

_____

STEP 7 If not, try some other ones – which ones will you try next? Do you need to think of some extra solutions?

_____

_____

_____

_____

_____

_____

STEP 8 Stop and remind yourself that it's great you have remembered to practise solving problems, no matter what the outcome.

How do you feel now?

_____

_____

_____

_____

_____

_____

Ideas for how to encourage and acknowledge my child's efforts:

Reward ideas

Things to say

My other responses

Things to do

Other ideas

My own treats for my efforts

My thought record

Situation – what's happening, where am I, who is there?

My thoughts – what am I thinking about in this situation? What am I predicting will happen? Do I have any memories, images about this?

Am I making any classic thinking errors? (e.g. predicting the worst, all or nothing thinking, fortune telling, etc.)

My feelings – How do I feel? What else am I feeling? Can I feel this in my body, what's that like?

My responses – what do I do/not do to cope with these thoughts and feelings?

Less helpful responses

Helpful responses

What are the real facts of the situation (that is, not based on how I feel or what I may be thinking)?

**Taking the facts into account, is there a more balanced way
I could think or see the situation?**

Does that make me feel differently? How do I feel now?

Does it help me to respond in more helpful ways? How?

What do I do? What's the outcome?

What have I learned that I might hold onto for the next time something like this comes up?

How will I remember this for next time?

Index